D0538311

PLANTS
AND
PLANT LIFE

VOLUME 7
Mosses and Ferns

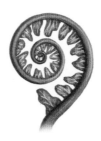

JILL BAILEY

GROLIER EDUCATIONAL

About this Set

PLANTS AND PLANT LIFE *is a ten-volume set that describes the world of plants in all its facets. Volume by volume, you will be introduced to the many different aspects of plant life.*

The first three volumes (1: Roots, Stems, and Leaves, 2: Flowers and Fruits, and 3: Life Processes) explain the basic structure, reproductive methods, and processes of life in flowering plants.

Volume 4 (Plant Ecology) explores the place of plants in the living community of life on Earth, while Volume 5 (Plants Used by People) presents the literally hundreds of plants that have been exploited by people for food, clothing, building, and many other uses.

The final five volumes (6: Algae and Fungi, 7: Mosses and Ferns, 8: Conifers, 9: Flowering Plants—The Monocotyledons, and 10: Flowering Plants—The Dicotyledons) lead the reader on a journey of discovery through the main groups of life that are usually classed as plants. In these volumes the typical and characteristic features of each group and its components are clearly outlined.

Though each volume deals with a distinct aspect of plant life, many of them are interrelated. To help you understand these links, every entry has enlightening cross-references to other entries and volumes. Throughout the set you will also find special short boxed features— entitled "Protecting Our World"—that focus on particular stories of environmental concern.

The whole set is liberally illustrated with diagrams explaining plant processes and structures, with depictions of typical plants and maps showing global distribution. In addition, hundreds of photographs bring the world of plants vividly to life. At the end of every volume there is a useful glossary explaining the technical terms that are used in the text, an index to all the volumes in the set, and finally, a list of other sources of reference (both books and websites). All the plants mentioned in the volume are listed alphabetically by common name, with their scientific names alongside.

Contents

Published 2001 by Grolier Educational,
Danbury, CT 06816

This edition published exclusively for the school
and library market

Planned and produced by Andromeda Oxford
Limited, 11–13 The Vineyard, Abingdon, Oxon
OX14 3PX, UK
www.andromeda.co.uk

Copyright © Andromeda Oxford Limited 2001

Project Director: *Graham Bateman*
Editorial Manager: *Peter Lewis*
Art Editors and Designers: *Martin Anderson,*
  Chris Munday, Steve McCurdy
Editors: *Penelope Isaac, Eleanor Stillwell*
Cartography: *Richard Watts, Tim Williams*
Editorial Assistant: *Marian Dreier*
Picture Manager: *Claire Turner*
Production: *Clive Sparling*
Index: *Ann Barrett*

Originated and printed in Hong Kong

**Library of Congress Cataloging-in-
Publication Data**

Plants and plant life.
    p.   cm.
    Includes bibliographical references.
    Contents: v.1. Roots, stems, and leaves --
v. 2. Flowers and fruits -- v. 3. Life processes
-- v. 4. Plant ecology -- v. 5. Plants used by people
-- v. 6. Algae and fungi -- v. 7. Mosses and ferns
-- v. 8. Conifers -- v. 9. Flowering plants--the
Monocotyledons -- v. 10. Flowering plants--the
Dicotyledons.
    ISBN 0-7172-9510-9 (set : alk. paper) --
ISBN 0-7172-9517-6 (vol. 7)
    1. Plants--Juvenile literature. 2. Botany--
Juvenile literature. [1.Plants--Encyclopedias.
2. Botany--Encyclopedias.] 1. Grolier Educational
Corporation.

QK49 .P54 2000
580--dc21
                                    99-056140

Set ISBN 0–7172–9510–9
Volume 7 ISBN 0–7172–9517–6

Liverworts HEPATOPHYTA

LIVERWORTS ARE OLDER than the dinosaurs. They have been spreading their green carpets across moist rocks and stream banks for over 350 million years. Today they are found from the poles to the tropics wherever there is a good supply of moisture for part of the year.

Liverworts were so named because many of them are shaped like a liver; *wort* is an old word for an herb. Liverworts are the simplest true plants on Earth. They do not have genuine stems, leaves, and roots, but only a very simple body, which is called the thallus (plural: thalli). There are no conducting tissues, such as xylem or phloem, and no air pores (stomata).

With no supporting tissues, liverworts cannot grow very tall. Tiny, hairlike structures known as rhizoids anchor them to soil, rocks, or tree bark, and help absorb moisture and minerals. Liverworts do not have waxy cuticles like flowering plants do, so water evaporates easily from their surface. They grow very close to the ground, trapping a layer of moisture that helps prevent them from drying out.

Liverworts may look rather small and dull, but they can do some surprising things. Some, such as *Frullania*, trap insects in tiny water-filled pitchers, just like carnivorous plants. Others contain

LIVERWORTS

Phylum:
Hepatophyta

NUMBER OF GENERA: c.225

NUMBER OF SPECIES:
6,000–8,000

DISTRIBUTION: worldwide, but most numerous in the tropics. Liverworts require at least one wet season a year and thrive best in permanently moist habitats

ECONOMIC USES: none, but readily colonize barren land after fires

symbiotic fungi that provide them with water and nutrients in return for food such as sugars.

Simple But Effective

There are two main forms of liverworts—thallose and leafy. The thallose liverworts are less complex. The plant body is made up of a simple sheet of cells, which may be branched or wavy, but has no obvious leaflike structures. Some thallose liverworts, such as *Sphaerocarpus*, are only about 0.04 inches (1 mm) in diameter.

One of the commonest thallose liverworts is *Pellia*. It grows along

the banks of streams and waterfalls, and in other moist, shady places. Its shining, dark-green thallus forks in two over and over again. *Pellia* is very easy to grow. You just need some moist soil, a shady place, and a fragment of thallus. A plastic bag over the pot will trap moist air while the fragment grows new rhizoids.

Not So Simple

Some liverworts are more complicated than they appear. *Marchantia*, for example, is a common liverwort that grows along stream banks, on mossy

▲ Sporophyte (spore capsules and slender stalks) and gametophyte (flat thallus) generations of *Pellia*.

▼ The "leaves" of *Peltigera* have no protective layer (cuticle), so it can survive only in moist places.

rocks, and among the ashes left after fires. Its branching fronds have wavy edges with midribs of thicker tissue. Only the upper part of the thallus contains chloroplasts, and hence is green. The lower part is colorless, and its cells store oil and other foods. Rows of scales under the thallus probably help trap moisture.

Just below the surface are many six-sided air-filled chambers. If you look closely at the surface, you can make out a hexagonal (six-sided) pattern. Each chamber contains strands of cells packed with chloroplasts, the sites of photosynthesis. A tiny hole opens to the outside, allowing carbon dioxide and oxygen to diffuse in and out. These pores stay open.

Some liverworts use air chambers for floating. *Riccia* floats at the surface of ponds and ditches.

Leafy Liverworts

Over 80 percent of all liverworts are leafy. They look like mosses, but are wetter and shinier. Unlike the leaves of mosses, their "leaves" do not contain any conducting cells and are only one cell thick. They are usually arranged in three rows—two obvious rows, plus a row of smaller leaves on the underside of the thallus. Often

LIFE CYCLE OF LIVERWORTS

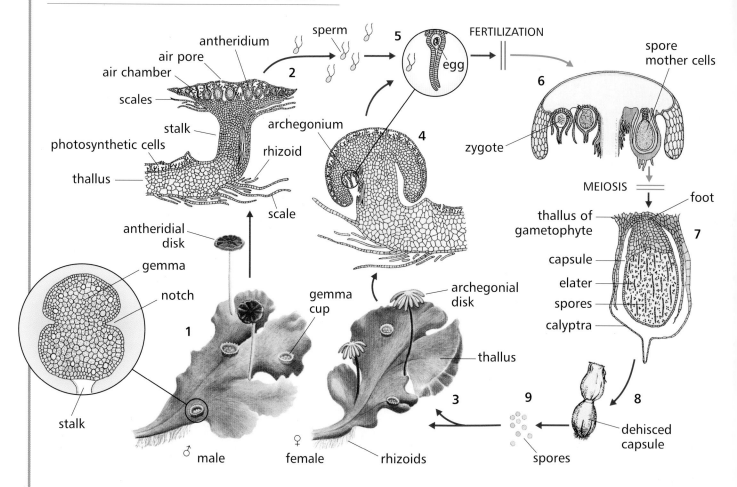

Liverworts, as well as mosses, differ from other plants in having only one set of chromosomes in the cells of the main plant body—in other words, they are haploid. Most plants have two sets. This haploid thallus is called the gametophyte ("gamete-bearing plant") generation because it will produce the gametes (sex cells)—the sperm and eggs. Each plant (thallus) is either male or female.

In *Marchantia*, shown here, strange, green, umbrellalike structures grow up from the surface of the thallus. On male thalli (1) they have a flat top. Embedded in it are several flask-shaped structures called antheridia (2). They produce the sperms. The female umbrellas (3) curve downward and have a series of fingerlike lobes. Under the umbrella there are more flasks—the archegonia (4), which produce the plant's eggs, one to each archegonium (5).

Splashes of rain carry the sperm to the female plants. Using a pair of tiny whiplike hairs (undulipodia), they swim through the film of moisture on the surface of the female plant to reach the eggs, attracted by special chemicals.

Each fertilized egg now forms a diploid zygote (6)—a cell with two sets of chromosomes, one set from the sperm and one from the egg. This cell then divides over and over again to produce an embryo, the sporophyte or "spore-bearing plant." It develops into a spore capsule on a short stalk or seta (7). The foot of the stalk is embedded in the gametophyte thallus and gets vital nutrients from it. The spores are produced from the spore mother cells by meiosis, a special kind of cell division that reduces the chromosome number back from two sets to one set.

Mixed in with the spores are very special structures called elaters. They are long, narrow, fiberlike cells with spirals of thickening on their walls. After the ripe capsule splits open and the lid (calyptra) is shed (8), the elaters absorb water and twist violently, flicking the spores out (9). They will germinate to produce new plants, either male or female. In many liverworts the sporophyte itself grows a long stalk to raise its spore capsule above the thallus.

the leaves are divided near the tip into two or more points.

Some leafy liverworts have evolved unusual ways of trapping moisture. Part of each leaf forms a small pitcher (urn), which catches water trickling down a tree trunk or rock face after a shower of rain.

The Multiplication Game

The way a liverwort reproduces can help you identify its species. Special structures for sexual reproduction provide obvious clues. *Marchantia* and its relatives produce umbrella-shaped structures on thick stalks, in which the sporophyte generation (see Life Cycle diagram left) develops after

▼ Gemma cups on a thallose liverwort. Each contains a cluster of tiny plantlets (gemmae) that will grow into new liverworts identical to their parents.

the egg is fertilized. Some liverworts produce their sporophytes under a flap of tissue. Most leafy liverworts wrap their developing spore capsules in a sheath formed from three fused leaves.

Many liverworts can also reproduce without sex. Tiny cups on the surface of the thallus contain lots of plantlets called gemmae, each a little two-lobed plate of cells attached by a weak stalk (see diagram left). Water splashes disperse the gemmae, and each grows into a new liverwort thallus identical to its parent. Some species, such as *Marchantia*, have round gemmae cups, while others, like *Lunularia*, have crescent-shaped ones.

As well as bearing gemmae, most liverworts can also reproduce by fragmentation—the thallus may be torn into two or more pieces, or part of it may rot away. The surviving part then continues to grow as an independent plant.

It is remarkable that such delicate, fragile plants should be important pioneers of newly exposed soil and rocks. Liverworts are often the first plants to colonize new areas, trapping moisture close to the ground. When they die and rot, they add valuable minerals and organic matter to the soil. Below their fronds is a sheltered microhabitat in which bacteria and other soil creatures can live.

See Also | *CELLULAR REPRODUCTION* **2** 40 | *VEGETATIVE REPRODUCTION* **2** 46 | *MOSSES* **7** 8 ◉

Mosses BRYOPHYTA

FROM THE TOPS of the tallest tropical jungle trees to the icy deserts of Antarctica, mosses form lush, green carpets. Their tiny, soft cushions appear in a variety of habitats—along the banks of streams, among the tiles of city roofs, and even in the cracks in sidewalks.

Mosses are small, rather simple plants that rarely grow bigger than 8 inches (20 cm) tall. Indeed, many measure less than 1 inch (2.5 cm). Some creep along the ground and over rocks in spreading mats, while others form tufts of tiny, upright plants.

What Is a Moss?

To the untrained eye mosses may all look quite similar to one another, but there are in fact over 14,500 different species. They have remained a significant part of the Earth's vegetation for almost 400 million years. So what is the secret of their success?

Mosses are more highly organized than liverworts. A moss plant is made up of a slender stem bearing whorls of simple leaves. Tiny threadlike structures called rhizoids anchor the plant in the soil. Although most moss leaves are only one cell thick, many species have a midrib (vein) that is several cells thick. This distinguishes mosses from leafy liverworts, which rarely have a midrib.

Mosses have air pores (stomata), but they are encircled by a single bagel-shaped cell, rather than the pair of guard cells in higher plants.

Mosses are better at taking up water than liverworts. In most species the rhizoids are made up of several cells (those of liverworts have only a single cell).

The stem contains a rather simple kind of conducting tissue —bundles of extralong cells that allow water to pass rapidly through them. These cells, called hydroids, lose their contents as they mature, rather like the xylem vessels of higher plants. They still

---

MOSSES

Phylum:
  Bryophyta (Musci)

NUMBER OF GENERA: c.660

NUMBER OF SPECIES: 14,500

DISTRIBUTION: worldwide, but mainly in moist places, especially in rainforests and bogs

ECONOMIC USES: mosses keep hanging baskets and cut flowers moist; peat (moss remains) used as fuel and in garden compost

◄ Mosses often grow in carpets containing several species, as in this colorful woodland group. Some form distinct plantlets, while others grow in close-knit tufts or mats.

False Mosses

Some "plants" that look like, and are called, mosses are not true mosses. The so-called reindeer moss that grows on the Arctic tundra and forms the main food of reindeer in winter is really a lichen. The club mosses are different again and are more like ferns than mosses. There are even a few algae—seaweeds—that are known by such names as "sea moss" and "Irish moss," probably because they grow close to the rocks on the seashore.

Saving Water

Like liverworts, most mosses have no waxy cuticle covering their leaves. They can absorb water over their whole surface, but they can easily lose water and dry out. This restricts them to moist habitats. A few species, however, do have a cuticle. Others contain special chemicals (colloids) in their cells that absorb water and hold on to it even under dry conditions.

Many mosses found in dry habitats, such as fringe mosses (*Grimmia*) and screw moss (*Tortula*), have fine, white, hairy points to their leaves, which make

keep their end walls, but they are very thin and readily allow water and dissolved materials to pass through them.

In a few hair-cap mosses (*Polytrichum* species) the hydroids are surrounded by other conducting cells (leptoids) that transport nutrients. These cells, in turn, are surrounded by a sheath of cells rich in stored starch.

Not all mosses are green or gray. The granite mosses (*Andreaea* species) that carpet the Arctic tundra are often black or brown, while some bog and peat mosses (*Sphagnum* species) may be a deep red or orange color. Usually these colors are due to special pigments (colored chemicals) that help protect the green chlorophyll from the sun's rays. But occasionally the strange colors that appear are the result of poor nutrition.

LIFE CYCLE OF MOSSES

Like liverworts, mosses have a life cycle that involves two different generations: a gametophyte generation, whose cells contain a single set of chromosomes (haploid), and a sporophyte generation with two sets of chromosomes in each cell (diploid). The moss plant most people see (1) is the gametophyte, which often (as here) is made up of hundreds of individual plants (2). Individual plants produce the sex cells (gametes)—the eggs and sperm—at the tip of the main shoot or on special side shoots. The eggs are produced in flask-shaped structures called archegonia (3). The sperm (antherozoids) are produced in simple oval sacs called antheridia (4). Archegonia and antheridia are mixed with threads called paraphyses and encircled by special leaves.

The sperm are dispersed (5) by raindrops. When they land on a female plant, they swim through the moisture on its surface using a pair of tiny whip-like undulipodia, attracted to the archegonia by a special chemical. The fertilized egg—the zygote—begins the sporophyte generation. The embryo (6) develops a foot that absorbs nutrients from inside the gametophyte parent plant, like a parasite. The rest of the embryo forms a spore capsule on a stalk, the seta (7). As the sporophyte grows, the remains of the archegonium form a cap over it, the calyptra (8). The seta and the base of the capsule can photosynthesize—they are green and have stomata. Inside the capsule (9) the sporophyte produces haploid spores by meiosis. Gradually, the

them look silvery or woolly. These hairy tips reflect the sun's heat, so reducing water loss from the leaf surface. Some other mosses get the same effect by having no green chlorophyll in the upper leaf cells, which lends them a silvery sheen.

A few mosses can survive years of drought by entering a resting stage. Others have spores that can withstand extreme drought. They will germinate to produce new moss plants after rain.

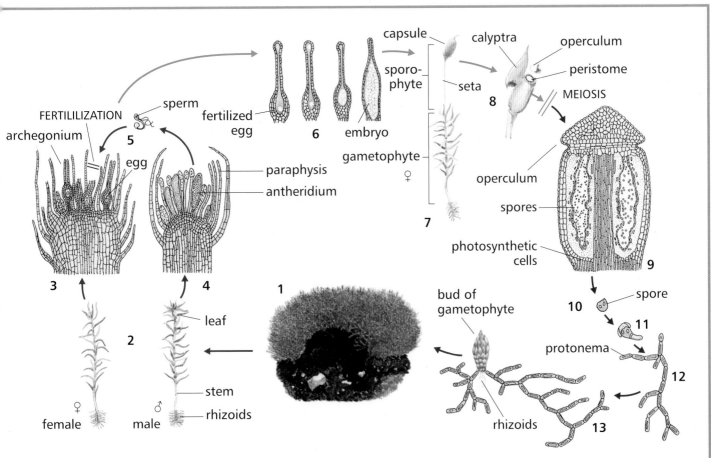

The life cycle diagram includes the following labels: capsule, calyptra, operculum, peristome, sporo-phyte, seta, MEIOSIS, 8, operculum, spores, photosynthetic cells, 9, FERTILIZATION, sperm, fertilized egg, archegonium, egg, 5, 6, embryo, gametophyte ♀, paraphysis, antheridium, 7, spore, 10, 11, protonema, 12, 1, bud of gametophyte, leaf, 2, stem, rhizoids, 13, female ♀, male ♂, 3, 4

capsule dries out and turns brown. A lid at the top (the operculum) opens, and the spores (10) are shaken out to be carried away on the breeze.

A single capsule may release as many as 50 million spores into the wind. These spores are the next generation of gameto-phytes. Each spore germinates

(11) to produce a branching green thread, which is called a protonema (12). Buds form at intervals on these threads and grow into new moss plants (13).

◀ The "saltshaker" teeth—the peristome at the tip of a capsule —only open to allow the release of spores, which are then carried away on the breeze.

Special Spore-shakers

Sexual reproduction in mosses first involves the production of male and female sex cells in special structures hidden in the tips of the stems. The fertilized egg grows into a capsule on a long stalk,

which can produce millions of spores. (See Life Cycle diagram above.) The capsules often appear as masses of pinlike structures sticking up above the green plants.

The capsules of mosses can help you identify them. Capsules and their stalks are often brightly colored. Capsules are round, cylindrical, or irregularly shaped. The capsules of *Splachnum* species, which grow on dung, are like little flared skirts. They seem to

act as airports for the many insects that visit dung to lay their eggs. The sticky spores brush off on visiting insects.

At the top of the spore capsule is a tiny lid. It opens to reveal a curious structure—one or more circles of little teeth, the peri-stome. These teeth control the release of spores, ensuring they are shed only when conditions are right for dispersal. The teeth respond to moisture in the air,

See Also | DISPERSAL OF FRUITS & SEEDS **2** 36 | EVOLUTION OF PLANTS **6** 4 | LIVERWORTS **7** 4 ◉

opening or closing with changes in humidity. When open, spores can escape through slits in an inner set of teeth, rather like a saltshaker.

Not all mosses have peristomes. The bog mosses just have a simple, hingelike lid on each capsule, while granite moss capsules split open into four valves, rather like liverwort capsules.

Asexual Reproduction

Mosses can multiply rapidly without producing eggs and sperm—they can undergo asexual (vegetative) reproduction. That is one reason why they are good at colonizing newly disturbed ground.

Some mosses produce little plantlets called gemmae on stalks at the tips of stems. Gemmae are dispersed by splashes of rain, and each may grow into a new moss plant. Other mosses produce plantlets called bulbils in the angles where the leaves join the stem or on underground rhizoids. In most species the thread that grows from a germinating spore—the protonema—itself produces many buds, each of which produces a moss plant. If parts of the protonema rot away, these plants become independent.

Become a Moss Detective

Mosses are extremely useful plants to the ecologist. Many species are very particular about where they

▲ Moss leaves are only one cell thick, except at the midrib, which contains bundles of long conducting cells.

grow. They can tell you a lot about the kind of rock, the acidity of the soil, the amount of rainfall, and the yearly temperature range of the area. In other words, mosses are valuable "indicator species."

Species of bog mosses, for example, signal that the ground is acidic and waterlogged, and definitely boggy. Be very careful before you step on a carpet of bog moss—you may sink deep into

the soggy ground, or worse! The bog moss may even be forming a floating carpet over deeper water.

If you come across granite mosses, you will know that the rocks they are growing on contain a lot of silica, so the soil is acidic. By contrast, screw moss (*Tortula*

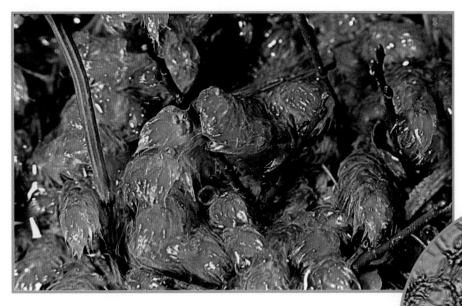

▲▼ In peat or bog mosses (*Sphagnum* species) normal photosynthesizing cells surround a series of chambers (gray in inset below) that hold water. *Sphagnum* mosses absorb water like sponges to form soft carpets and mounds.

muralis), a bright green moss that becomes grayish-colored and twisted when dry, grows mainly on calcareous (limy) rocks and walls.

If you find a very common bright green cord moss (*Funaria hygrometrica*), you will know that the soil contains plenty of nutrients. *Funaria* is especially common on the sites of old campfires, where wood ash has enriched the soil. It is also often found on city sidewalks and has been called "a weed of the world." If you find some *Funaria* that has bright orange fruiting capsules, try wetting it: the capsule stalks will twist and spin.

Splachnum species are spectacular bright yellow or red mosses whose capsules are like little, curving skirts. If you find these mosses, you can be sure that there is dung around. They are particularly fond of growing on moose droppings.

Moss-hunting

Mosses are not the easiest plants to identify. If you want to learn the secrets mosses can tell you, you will need to get a good hand lens or magnifying glass and a field guide to mosses with high-quality color photographs. It is well worth making the effort—you will be surprised at the beauty of these tiny plants when you see them close up.

When collecting mosses, it is best to transport them in paper bags, not plastic. They rot and disintegrate very quickly in humid surroundings. You will need a notebook to record where and at what time of year you collected your specimens. What were they growing on? Soil, rock, tree bark, or walls, for example. Did they form tufts or creeping mats? Are the little plantlets upright, or do they form flattish feathery fronds?

If you want to identify mosses accurately, you must describe the shape and measure the length of stems and leaves, note whether there is a midrib, and whether a hair point extends beyond the tip of the leaf. The color is a useful guide, too. It is interesting to look at your moss specimen both dry and wet—as well as changes in color, you may well notice some dramatic curling and twisting of the leaves. If the moss is fruiting, make a note of the length of the capsules and their stalks, their shape and color, and whether the stalks are straight or twisted.

The names of mosses are quite a challenge. They are such tiny,

inconspicuous plants that very few have been given common names. The Latin names are rather complicated, but it helps if you try to find out what they mean.

Each moss species has two names. The second name tells you what the particular species is, while the first is the genus (group) that it belongs to. The species name is often very revealing. Take *Tortella tortuosa*, for instance, which is often found growing on limestone—the word *tortuosa* means "twisted" and refers to the way the leaves curl up when dry.

Polytrichum species have easily understood names. *P. commune* is the "common" one; *P. piliferum* is whitish-colored, with fine hairy tips to the leaves (from the Latin word *pili*, which means "hairs"); *P. gracile* is a slender ("graceful") form; *P. alpinum* is an alpine species, and *P. nanum* a dwarf species (from the Latin word *nanum*, meaning "dwarf").

The Bog Makers

Peat or bog mosses belong to the genus *Sphagnum*. They grow in boggy places—in fact, they can even create bogs! Peat mosses are like living sponges; they absorb water and hold it in special chambers formed from dead, thickened cells in the leaves. These mosses are capable of holding more than 20 times their own dry weight of water. In areas of high rainfall where the rocks do not allow water to drain away easily, peat moss bogs can cover vast areas. The Great Dismal Swamp on the border between North Carolina and Virginia now covers some 750 square miles (1,940 sq. km) but once spread over an astonishing

◀ **Peat or bog mosses (*Sphagnum* species) form vast bogs in areas of impermeable rocks in wet climates. Layers of peat formed can be many feet deep.**

▲ **Peat is cut and used as fuel in many parts of the world. This commercial peat-digging operation is in Connemara, in the Republic of Ireland.**

2,200 square miles (5,700 sq. km). Many peat bogs in Europe, especially in Scotland and Ireland, formed where early man cut down the forests, leaving thin, bare soils over acidic rocks in a wet climate.

Beware of walking on peat bogs—the ground may be very treacherous. Peat mosses growing on a lakeshore may gradually invade the lake, forming a thick, floating mat that looks deceptively like solid ground. People and animals that tread on such a "quaking bog" can easily sink through the mat into the deep water below and drown, unable to claw their way back to the surface through many feet of moss.

In the peat bogs of northern North America (the "muskegs"), mosses often form hummocks, as layers of new moss build up on the dead remains of earlier plants. Gradually, as the bog rises, it gets drier, and other plants invade.

Peat mosses can be very colorful. In places like the Arctic tundra and high mountains, where the light is intense and ultraviolet radiation strong, many peat mosses are deep red or orange. These colors come from special pigments that screen the cells from damage by the high radiation.

From Heating to Healing

Peat moss has many economic uses. Peat itself is formed from the remains of peat mosses. The water in a peat bog is very acidic, and air cannot readily circulate around the bog, so few bacteria survive, and the moss does not rot down much. Instead, it accumulates until the weight of moss compacts it to form peat. Peat is used all

HORNWORTS

Hornworts are tiny plants rather like liverworts. Their cells contain just one large chloroplast, with a special starch-storing structure called a pyrenoid. Pyrenoids are common in green algae, but unknown in other plants. Hornworts are named for their long, horn-shaped spore capsules, which may be up to 2 inches (5 cm) tall. They are green and photosynthetic, with stomata and a cuticle, like the sporophytes of mosses. When ripe, the capsules split into two valves that twist as humidity changes, flicking out the spores. Most species also have elaters, like liverworts. The

leafy lobes of many hornworts have chambers full of cyanobacteria that trap atmospheric nitrogen and convert it into nitrates for the hornwort. This helps them grow on bare rock surfaces. Hornworts have their own phylum (Anthocerophyta).

over the world as a fuel. It smolders slowly and steadily, giving off quite a pleasant odor.

Gardeners and commercial growers use peat to make a compost that holds water well. Peat moss is also an effective dressing for wounds—it keeps out air and contains iodine, which acts as a disinfectant. Peat dressings were used for soldiers in World War I.

Global Citizens

Mosses play a vital role in the planet's ecosystems. By colonizing bare ground, tree bark, rocks, and other bare surfaces, they start the process of soil formation. Some

mosses can survive with very few nutrients, so long as they have a little light and plenty of moisture. This is because they grow slowly.

Moss cushions and mats trap particles of dust and organic material blown on the wind. As the cushions grow larger, older mosses die and rot away, adding to the organic matter trapped around them. The rotting material is acidic and helps wear away the rock or other surface below, adding minerals to the young soil. On the branches of high forest trees thick carpets of mosses provide a base for larger ferns, club mosses, and orchids to take

hold, creating aerial gardens high above the forest floor.

Many insects and other small creatures find shelter and food among the mosses. They in turn attract small mammals and birds, which feed on them. The mosses form a carpet that helps trap moisture in the soil, where it can benefit larger plants such as trees, which tower above the mosses.

Gardeners use mosses to help prevent water evaporating from hanging baskets and planters. Florists use it to wrap around flowers that are being sent long distances. Moss can be reused like a bath sponge—when it has lost its water, it can be wetted again and again.

Next time you take a walk, look out for these lowly plants. Even in the city you can find them in sidewalks, on roof tiles and old logs, and in damp backyards. See how many different kinds you can spot. Look at them in wet weather and dry weather, and note any changes. Do they change color? Do the leaves curl or uncurl? Watch for the golden brown spore capsules, and see how they push the shaggy calyptras off as they grow.

▶ **Mosses thrive in damp places where sunlight is not too intense. They can completely cover rocks, starting a cycle of colonization by other plants.**

Prehistoric Plants

THE GREAT COAL SWAMPS of the Carboniferous period flourished in a warm, humid climate. Giant ferns, horsetails, and club mosses grew so quickly and in such abundance that their remains piled up on the floor of the swamp forest faster than they could rot away. Over many millennia they were turned into coal.

The earliest plant fossils date back over 400 million years. The Carboniferous period, between 354 and 295 million years ago, was the heyday of mosses and ferns. At this time tree-sized ferns and club mosses formed vast forests, giant horsetails dominated the swamps, while a luxuriant carpet of mosses and smaller ferns, horsetails, and club mosses covered the land. As this era was drawing to a close, a new group of plants—the seed plants—made their appearance, including the very earliest cycads, ginkgoes, and conifers.

The First Plants

The oldest fossil plants are forking stems just a few inches long with spore sacs at their tips (e.g., *Aglaophyton, Zosterophyllum, Horneophyton,* and *Psilophyton*). These simple plants had no leaves, just green stems with air pores (stomata) anchored in the soil by tiny rhizoids. They were restricted to moist habitats and did not grow very big, since they had no woody tissues. When they died, fungi and bacteria broke down their remains, forming the first soil. As soils developed, they were able to support bigger plants.

These early plants did not have proper roots. Instead, they formed a partnership (symbiosis) with fungi to help them take up nutrients. Wrapped around rhizoids or even inside stems and rhizoids, the fungi took up minerals and turned them into nutrients the plants could use. In return they received carbohydrates made by the plants in photosynthesis.

▼ The earliest land plants were just branching green stems bearing spore sacs. Ancestors of the club mosses (*Asteroxylon*) bore the first leaves.

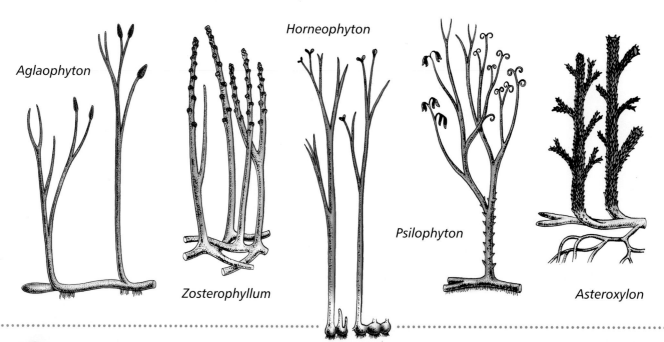

Aglaophyton

Zosterophyllum

Horneophyton

Psilophyton

Asteroxylon

▶ Fossil leaves of an early seed plant from the Carboniferous period.

Eventually, ancestors of the club mosses (e.g., *Asteroxylon*) appeared, with tiny leaves (microphylls) that greatly increased the surface area for photosynthesis. They had well-developed conducting tissues with tracheids, which allowed the plants to transport water and nutrients farther, so they could grow taller. With the arrival of the ferns, with their much bigger leaves (megaphylls), the scene was set for the growth of trees and other large land plants.

Giants of the Coal Swamps

The Carboniferous period was a warm period, in which vast swamps and humid forests flourished. But the forest trees were unlike any in existence today—they were giant club mosses, horsetails, and ferns. They had very little true woody tissue, but found support in other ways. Some had thick bark and layers of fibrous tissues just below it. The tree ferns had a massive cortex and layers of tough leaf bases.

Some of these trees were very large. The giant club mosses, such as *Lepidodendron* and *Sigillaria*, grew up to 100 feet (30 m) tall. *Calamites*, a treelike horsetail, may

have been the largest plant that has ever lived. It had a creeping rhizome that produced many shoots, each of which grew into a tree up to 65 feet (20 m) tall. Unlike present-day trees, however, there were strict limits on how big *Calamites* could grow. It would reach a certain size, then reproduce and die.

In this humid climate growth was so rapid that plant remains did not have time to rot away before they were covered by more plant remains. As they were buried, fewer bacteria and fungi could act on them, and they began to build up. Over millions of years the great pressure of these accumulating sediments, together with heat (which increases as you sink deeper into the Earth), compacted them into coal.

PROTECTING OUR WORLD

COAL AND GLOBAL WARMING

Coal is one of the main fossil fuels in the modern world. The ancient plants from which coal was formed once trapped carbon dioxide during photosynthesis. When we burn coal, the carbon dioxide is released again into the atmosphere. The earth gets vital heat from the sun, but must also reflect a lot back to avoid overheating. But carbon dioxide absorbs and holds in this reflected heat, just like the panes of glass in a greenhouse. Global warming is the result, which scientists link to climate change and an alarming rise in world sea levels.

See Also | *PLANTS & GLOBAL CLIMATE* **4** *34* | *CLUB MOSSES* **7** *22* | *HORSETAILS* **7** *28* 👁

PREHISTORIC LANDSCAPE

▼ A swamp scene from the late Carbon-iferous period, around 250 million years ago. This era was the heyday of mosses, ferns, and their relations. Tree-sized club mosses (1 *Lepidodendron*, 2 *Sigillaria*), ferns (3 *Psaronius*), and horsetails (4 *Cala-mites*) dominate the landscape, which is carpeted in smaller mosses (5), club mosses (6), ferns (7, 8), and horsetails (9, 10, 11). Early coniferlike trees such as *Cordaites* (12) were also present. Over millions of years the remains of many of these plants were compacted into coal. The fauna of the period was represented by insects and other arthropods and amphibians, some as big as alligators.

Club Mosses LYCOPHYTA

CLUB MOSSES ARE DESCENDED from giant forest trees that dominated the Carboniferous coal swamps over 300 million years ago. Modern club mosses, which are far smaller than their ancestors, look like dwarf conifers. Some—the tassel ferns—form dense, green curtains that drape over the branches of tropical trees.

Club mosses are not mosses at all—they are plants with properly developed tissues that transport water and nutrients around the plant (xylem and phloem) and true leaves and roots. Plants with xylem and phloem are called vascular plants. Club mosses have small, glossy leaves called microphylls with just a single vein down the middle. Like ferns, club mosses and their allies do not bear flowers or seeds, but reproduce by spores. Yet, unlike ferns, they produce only one spore sac (sporangium) on each of the fertile leaves, and it is always at the base of the leaf.

As in all vascular plants, the main plant you see is the sporophyte generation—the plant that will produce spores. The gametophyte, which makes the eggs and sperm, is much smaller, and in club mosses is often underground.

There are three groups of club mosses and their allies: the true

CLUB MOSSES

Phylum: Lycophyta

NUMBER OF GENERA: 6

NUMBER OF SPECIES: about 1,230

DISTRIBUTION: worldwide, from the high mountains of the Andes to American deserts and lake beds; most species are found in tropical rainforests

ECONOMIC USES: houseplants, homeopathic remedies and other medicinal uses; spores once used in photo flashes and fireworks

◀ **Trees draped in club mosses in the Olympic National Park rainforest, Washington State.**

club mosses, the spike-mosses, and the grasslike quillworts that grow around and even in lakes and ponds. Club mosses and spike-mosses are sometimes grouped together and called lycopods (from the Greek words *lukos*, meaning "wolf," and *pous*, meaning "foot")—their branching was thought to look like a wolf's foot.

True Club Mosses

Club mosses are small, evergreen plants with many small, almost triangular leaves arranged in rows around the stem. In many species these rows are so regular that they make the plant look braided. The stems repeatedly fork in two. The sole exception is a tiny plant called *Phylloglossum*, just 2 inches (5 cm) tall, which has a spiral of spike-shaped succulent leaves.

The name club moss comes from the fertile shoots, which bear the spore sacs (sporangia). Spore sacs develop at the base of special leaves called sporophylls. In most species the sporophylls are grouped together at the tips of branches, forming club-shaped cones or tassels (strobili).

See Also | CELL TYPES & TISSUES *1* 18 | PREHISTORIC PLANTS *7* 18 ◉

There are many club mosses in North America and Europe. Fir club mosses form small bunches of upright stems barely 8 inches (20 cm) tall that look like small clumps of miniature pine trees. The ground pines (or ground cedars) of American woodlands are used in Christmas decorations. Many club mosses are grown as houseplants. Some have striking foliage in shades of yellow, green, and even blue.

Tough Pioneers

Although most club moss species live in the tropics, there are many species in cooler climates. Some are pioneer species in the harsh environment of high mountains. Their creeping underground stems are protected from the

▲ **Spore-bearing cones of a club moss have special scalelike leaves (sporophylls) with kidney-shaped spore sacs at their bases.**

extremes of temperature and wind by the soil and low-growing plants. They may spread out to form colonies many feet across. The running pine is named for its widely creeping stems that run over the ground. Even if parts of the creeping stem die, the upright shoots can put down roots and become independent plants.

In the high Andes of South America bushlike clumps of *Lycopodium* species have to cope with high light intensity by day and freezing temperatures by night. The thick cuticle of club moss leaves helps reduce water

LIFE CYCLE OF LYCOPODIUM

The club moss you see in the wild is the sporophyte generation (1); each cell contains two sets of chromosomes. The upright shoots arise from creeping underground rhizomes. When mature, the sporophyte produces spores in little sacs called sporangia at the bases of special leaves, called sporophylls. In many species the sporophylls are arranged in whorls, forming cones (or strobili) at the tips of branches (2). In others, sporophylls are mixed with ordinary leaves. Inside the sacs spores are produced by meiosis of the spore mother cells (3), so each spore has only one set of chromosomes. When ripe, the spore sacs (4) split open, and the tiny spores (5) are carried away on the breeze.

Club mosses produce just one kind of spore. The spore germinates to form the gametophyte generation (6). In a few species it is a tiny, green, cup-shaped structure that lasts only a few months. In others it is a rounded or carrot-shaped underground tuber (7), anchored by tiny roots. These tubers are colorless and have fungi living in their outer tissues, which help supply them with nutrients. They may survive underground for many years. Sometimes parts of a

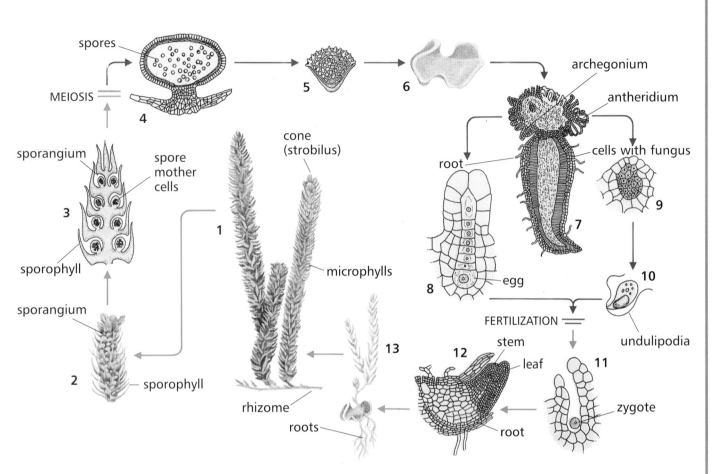

spores

MEIOSIS

4

5

6

archegonium

antheridium

sporangium

spore mother cells

3

sporophyll

sporangium

2

sporophyll

1

cone (strobilus)

microphylls

rhizome

roots

13

12

stem

leaf

root

root

cells with fungus

9

egg

8

FERTILIZATION

10

undulipodia

11

zygote

gametophyte tuber rot away, and the remaining parts become separate plants, a form of vegetative reproduction. If conditions are bad, the gametophyte may even produce gemmae, tiny plantlets that develop into new plants.

Eventually, the gametophyte produces the female archegonia and male antheridia on spreading

▶ Spores from the staghorn club moss (lycopodium powder). Lycopodium powder used to be ignited as photography flashes and in fireworks, and was also used in medicinal skin powders and for coating pills.

lobes near the soil surface. Each archegonium (8) contains an egg, and within the antheridium (9) a cluster of cells develops that form sperm with long undulipodia (10). The little sperm swim in the soil moisture to fertilize the eggs to form a zygote (11). Then the new sporophyte generation starts to grow in the archegonium. It develops a "foot" that absorbs food from the parent plant. The other end of the embryo develops into the first root, stem, and leaf (12). Once the shoot has grown up into the sunlight (13), photosynthesis takes over, and the gametophyte shrivels away.

See Also | *THE WORLD'S BIOMES 4 36* | *EVOLUTION OF PLANTS 6 4*

LIFE CYCLE OF SELAGINELLA

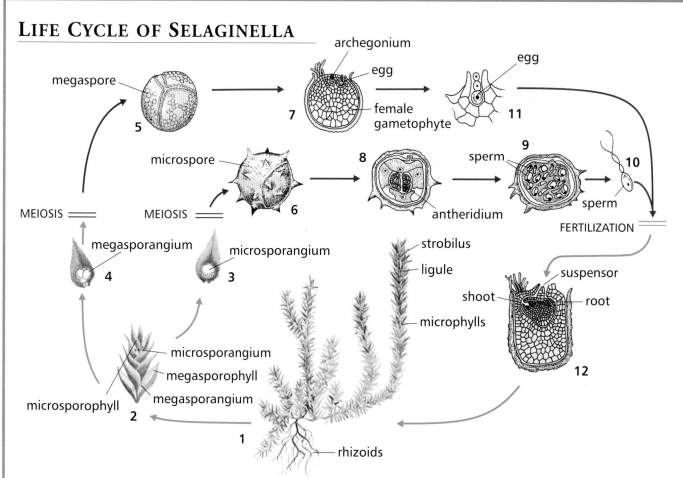

The life cycle of *Selaginella* is similar to that of *Lycopodium*. The plant we see here (1) is the spore-producing or sporophyte generation. *Selaginella* produces two kinds of spores at the shoot tips (2), which give rise to separate male and female gametophyte plants. Usually the male spore sacs (3; microsporangia) develop near the tip of each cone on tiny leaves (microsporophylls). The female spore sacs (4; megasporangia) develop further down on larger leaves (megasporophylls). Megasporangia each produce a few large megaspores (5), some of the biggest in the plant kingdom.

When swollen with food, they may be over 0.04 inches (1 mm) in diameter. They will grow into female gametophytes, fed by the rest of the tissue in the spore sac. Microsporangia produce many more small, dustlike spores, the microspores (6), which produce the male gametophytes.

The spores begin to germinate while still on the parent plant. The gametophyte stage is much more delicate and lasts a much shorter time than in *Lycopodium*. This makes *Selaginella* less dependent on moist conditions. The female gametophyte is a small green lobe of tissue containing archegonia (7). It grows by

absorbing food from the parent plant. The male gametophyte is made up of just a few cells and an antheridium (8). Once the spores are shed, the microspores (9) split open to release the sperm (10). The megaspores split to expose the female gametophytes, which grow out like little cushions. Archegonia (11) nestle in this cushion, surrounded by rhizoids that may help trap water for the sperm to swim in. The fertilized egg develops directly into an embryo plant (12). A band of tissue known as the suspensor develops; it pushes the embryo down into the food reserve.

loss by day and provides some insulation against the cold at night. Many of these plants are bright red or yellow, since they produce colorful pigments that screen the leaves from the damaging ultraviolet rays of the sun. Long hairs at the tips of the leaves in some club mosses also help reduce evaporation (transpiration) and insulate against the cold. The hairs give the plants a whitish color, since they reflect the sun's rays rather than absorb them.

The Spike-mosses

Spike-mosses (*Selaginella* species) are found mostly in the tropics. They range from small plants that trail down from the branches of trees to large climbers. The stems fork repeatedly. The leaves may spiral around the stem or may lie in the same plane as the branches, forming flattened, fernlike fronds.

Each leaf has a tiny tongue-shaped scale (ligule) on its upper side close to the stem. They shrivel as the leaf matures and perhaps produce water to keep the young leaves and sporangia moist.

Selaginella has some special features. Sometimes the water-conducting tracheids in the stem have no end walls and become

◀ Some *Selaginella* species have two rows of large, flattened leaves, with smaller leaves above, pressed closely against the stem.

continuous tubes like xylem vessels. Then there are the rhizophores—proplike structures that grow down beside branches of the stem and fork before growing into the soil. If they break off from the main plant, they can grow new leafy branches.

Many spike-mosses are grown as houseplants. Some unusual ones, such as the aptly named resurrection plants, are sold as novelties. Native to the deserts of the southern United States and Mexico, they roll up tightly into a ball of "dead" fronds—only to uncurl, turn green again, and start to grow after rain! Even when they really are dead, they will curl and uncurl with changes in humidity.

WHISK FERNS (PSILOPHYTA)

Whisk ferns are the simplest of vascular plants. They look like the earliest land plants from 400 million years ago, known to us from fossils. They have no true leaves or roots, only upright green stems that fork repeatedly in two. These stems have stomata and photosynthesize. The vascular tissue in the stems has xylem made up of tracheids, and the phloem has only poorly developed sieve cells. Whisk ferns are anchored by creeping underground rhizomes that bear tiny rhizoids. Like the roots of many conifers and flowering plants, the rhizoids contain symbiotic fungi that provide them with soil nutrients. Tiny branches in the angle between scale leaves and the stem make little sacs of spores. They germinate to produce small, branching, rhizome-like gametophytes that live underground or in the crevices of tree bark. Like the rhizoids of the sporophyte generation, the outer cells of the whisk fern gametophytes also contain fungi.

See Also | WATER & WATER UPTAKE **3** 24 | SURVIVING EXTREMES **3** 42

Horsetails SPHENOPHYTA

HORSETAILS ARE SO CALLED because their jointed stems and whorls of slender branches are thought to resemble the hairs of a horse's tail. Today's horsetails are rather inconspicuous plants, but their tree-sized ancestors were prominent in forests 300 million years ago. Looking at a patch of horsetails is like looking at an ancient landscape in miniature.

Horsetails reproduce by spores and have special conducting cells in their stems—they are vascular plants. Species of the Arctic tundra and high mountains may be little more than an inch (2.5 cm) high, while some large tropical horsetails grow up to 30 feet (10 m) tall. The largest of all, the South American giant horsetail, may be tall, but it is less than ¾ inch (2 cm) in diameter and cannot support its own weight. It clambers over nearby trees like a vine. The giant horsetail, or great horsetail, that grows beside streams and swamps and in wet forests in North America and Europe is often 6 feet (2 m) high.

The common horsetail is one of the ten commonest plants in the world. It spreads rapidly over open fields and moist places, and along roadsides. Horsetails usually have permanent underground stems, which produce shoots that die back in winter or during a dry season. This helps them survive even in dry places. Because these stems run deep down into the soil, they are very difficult to root out when the plants colonize cultivated land. A few species of horsetail are evergreen.

Scouring Rushes

A common name for horsetails is scouring rushes. That is because their stems are rough with deposits of silica, a hard glassy substance. This substance makes them tough enough to scour pots with—medieval Europeans, Native Americans, and campers have used these plants as pot-scourers. The stems of some species are even used to polish wood.

The stems have ridges that run down from each leaf to the node below. They are produced by strips of tough sclerenchyma cells, cells with extrathick walls, which in this case contain silica for added strength. Because they are so rough, clumps of tall horsetails can hold each other up, since their stems are too rough to slide past each other!

Most horsetail stems are jointed—they have hollow centers, broken by bands of tissue at each node. The hollow core is surrounded by a ring of vascular bundles (xylem and phloem). The xylem consists mainly of tracheids,

HORSETAILS

Phylum:
  Sphenophyta

NUMBER OF GENERA: 1

NUMBER OF SPECIES: 15

DISTRIBUTION: common in temperate climates, especially North America, Europe, and Asia. Not found in Australia

ECONOMIC USES: used in herbal medicine to treat liver and eye complaints, and in cosmetics

◄ The giant or great horsetail, the largest species in North America and Europe, grows up to 6 feet (2 m) tall. This vegetative shoot shows the whorls of side branches that arise from nodes just above the scale leaves.

not vessels. The phloem sieve cells have no companion cells. Outside the vascular bundles is a ring of long, vertical air canals, which lie under the grooves between the surface ridges.

Doing without Leaves

Horsetail stems appear almost leafless. The leaves are very small, wedge-shaped structures with a single vein down the middle and are sometimes called microphylls. These leaves have given their name to the group (phylum) to which horsetails belong, the Sphenophyta (from the Greek words *sphen*, meaning "wedge," and *phuton*, meaning "plant").

The leaves arise just below the nodes and form a sheath around the stem, adding to the jointed look. The leaves often have dark bands at their bases or tips. As they grow older, they become dry and scaly.

By having very small leaves and using their stems for photosynthesis, horsetails have a relatively small surface area over which to lose water by transpiration. The air pores (stomata) are sunk in

LIFE CYCLE OF HORSETAILS

Like mosses and ferns, horsetails produce spores rather than seeds. These spores germinate into a tiny gametophyte generation that produces sperm and eggs. The fertilized eggs grow into a sporophyte, the plant familiar to us.

Horsetails produce their spores in conelike structures at the tips of shoots (1). Some species have separate cone-bearing shoots, called fertile shoots. The cones (2) are made up of whorls of little scaly leaves, the sporangiophores, which are often six-sided. The spore-sacs, or sporangia, hang down from them.

▲ The vegetative and fertile shoots of the common horsetail.

Inside the sporangia (3) the horsetail produces spores by meiosis, so the spores have only one set of chromosomes. When the spores are ripe, the sporangia split open and release them into the air currents. Horsetail spores are green and delicate, and survive for only a few days.

Four thick, ribbonlike strips with spoon-shaped tips grow out from the wall of each spore like a cross. These "elaters" wrap around the spore until it is released (4). Then they uncoil (5) and dry out, flicking the spores away from the parent plant. They

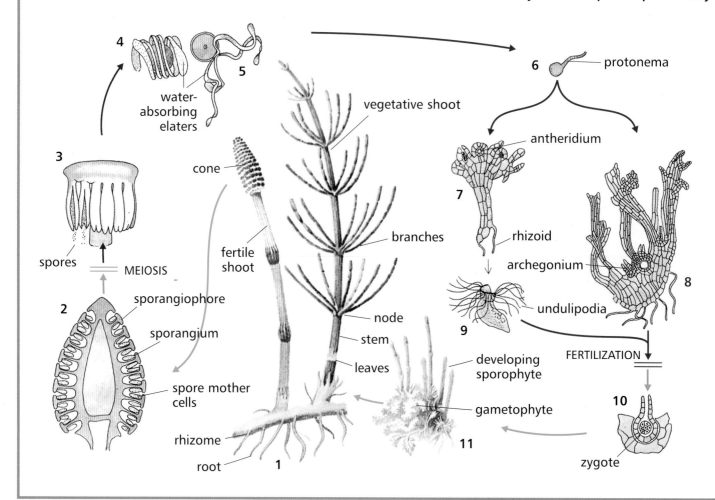

also help spores cling to each other. This makes sure that when the tiny spores germinate to form little gametophyte plants, they will be close enough together for the sperm to swim to the eggs.

When a spore germinates (6), it produces a little green filament rather like a moss protonema. It soon becomes a cushion of cells anchored by tiny rhizoids. Some spores produce a small yellowish-green male gametophyte (7), which is rarely more than ½ inch (1 cm) across. The gametophyte produces the male antheridia, which in turn produce sperm. Other spores produce a larger, dark green gametophyte that generates first antheridia and later the female archegonia (8). Using a crown of tiny beating hairs known as undulipodia (9), the sperm swim in a film of moisture to the eggs in the archegonia. Each fertilized egg, or zygote (10), grows into a new sporophyte plant. At first, it absorbs food from the parent gametophyte (11), but soon it puts out a root and leaves and becomes independent. The root soon dies as the creeping stem puts down adventitious roots instead. If several eggs are fertilized, a number of new sporophytes grow from the same gametophyte.

▲ New sporophyte plants grow out from the spongelike gametophyte of the water horsetail.

the grooves between the stem ridges, which trap the moisture leaving the plant. This slows down the rate of water loss.

Creeping Clumps

Many horsetails grow in clumps. Sometimes they cover vast areas such as roadside banks. The shoots grow up from thick underground stems called rhizomes. The rhizomes branch and produce more shoots from their nodes. They also send down thinner roots known as adventitious roots.

If part of a rhizome rots away, the remaining parts become independent plants identical to their neighbors. Trampled horsetails that break into fragments can put down roots and become new plants. Occasionally the pieces may be swept away in streams

and a new population begins to grow some distance downstream. Some horsetails grow tubers on special side roots. The tubers break off to become new plants.

Gold Miners

Horsetails take up gold from water and concentrate it in their tissues. However, you will not get very rich extracting gold from horsetails—at best 2.2 pounds (1 kg) of horsetails will yield only 0.0088 ounces (0.25 g) of the precious metal! But at least testing horsetails for gold can tell you whether gold is present in the soil or rocks below.

Horsetails have other uses, too. There are many ancient and

modern medicines that derive from horsetails. The rough horsetail, or common scouring rush, is harvested in Norway and China for its silica, which is used to treat liver complaints. The common horsetail is used to treat painful joints in Malaysia and sore mouths in the Caribbean. Extracts of horsetail stems are widely sold in the United States to smooth away wrinkles and tone up nails, hair, and skin. Traditional folk medicine has also found many uses for horsetails. For example, they are claimed to heal bones, perhaps because they are rich in calcium. Horsetails are also thought to be effective in treating ulcers and acne, and in helping infertile women become pregnant. A possible treatment for Alzheimer's disease is being explored, too. They are also ingredients in many modern cosmetics.

Some more unusual applications of horsetails include using the stems of the common horsetail to make reeds for clarinets, drying the stems of the wood horsetail to make a yellow dye, and using the stems of the giant horsetail as mantles for gaslights. Some Native Americans of the Pacific Northwest (around Vancouver) weave baskets from the fibers of these stems.

▲ ▶ Horsetails grow in various habitats. The water horsetail (above right) grows around lakes. Its stems have few branches near the base, to allow for fluctuations in water level. A large air canal occupies most of the stem, which allows oxygen to reach the roots in the mud below the water. The common horsetail (top left) can grow in dry habitats like these dunes. Here, pinkish cone-bearing fertile shoots mingle with occasional green vegetative shoots. Horsetails can even be found on city lots (bottom left).

A Deadly Delicacy

The boiled young shoots of horse-tails are eaten all over the world as a vegetable, rather like asparagus. Native Americans are recorded as having eaten them, as well as ancient Romans and ancient Britons. However, horsetails can be extremely poisonous. Many cattle and horses have died after eating them. The problem is a chemical (enzyme) that breaks down other vital chemicals (the vitamin thiamine) in the body.

Because of their ability to put down extensive roots and spread rapidly, horsetails can become very troublesome weeds in a garden. It is difficult to dig them up without leaving a fragment of stem behind in the ground, and that is all a horsetail needs to grow a new plant and begin spreading all over again.

See Also | *SURVIVING EXTREMES* **3** *42* | *FIBERS* **5** *34* | *MEDICINAL PLANTS* **5** *42* 👁

Ferns FILICINOPHYTA

FERNS ARE GREAT SURVIVORS, growing in a wide range of habitats around the world—from hot deserts to cold tundra. Some even thrive high up in the canopy of the tropical rainforest.

Ferns range from low-growing herbs to treelike forms. They have true stems and roots. Their leaves, called fronds or megaphylls, are arranged in spirals. Ferns do not have extra thickening like some flowering plants, so do not produce much woody tissue, which limits their size.

Flowerless Ferns

Ancient folklore claimed that on Midsummer's Eve, ferns produced invisible, short-lived flowers with invisible seeds! In fact, ferns have no flowers or cones at all; they produce spores within sacs (sporangia), which develop directly on the fronds.

Like club mosses and horsetails, most ferns have creeping underground stems (rhizomes) with thin adventitious roots. New shoots grow from the rhizomes, and a single fern can colonize a huge area. Tree ferns have fat, almost vertical rhizomes. Other ferns form branching tufts. Filmy ferns have hardly any roots and rely solely on root hairs to take up water. Many ferns die back in winter or in a dry season, then use food that they have stored in the rhizome to grow new shoots when conditions improve.

From Fiddleheads to Fronds

Most fern leaves are coiled up as they push through the soil. This protects the delicate growing tip. Since the coiled fronds look like the scrolls on violins, they have been nicknamed "fiddleheads."

Typically, fern fronds are large leaves covered in a waterproof, waxy cuticle and with many air pores (stomata). Below the top layer (epidermis) there is a layer of green photosynthesizing cells, and below them are storage cells containing lots of starch.

Each frond is made up of a blade and a leaf stalk (the stipe). A branching web of veins carries food and water to the leaf. Many fern fronds are divided into leaflets called pinnae, and often the pinnae divide into even smaller leaflets (pinnules). The part of the leaf stalk to which the leaflets are attached is called the rachis.

Color and Scent

Ferns come in many shades of green, and even red and purple. Some ferns have black, brown, or

---

FERNS

Phylum:
  Filicinophyta

NUMBER OF FAMILIES: 33

NUMBER OF GENERA: 223

DISTRIBUTION: worldwide, present in most habitats but especially diverse in the tropics and subtropics

ECONOMIC USES: starchy stems are edible when cooked; all parts are used in herbal medicines; fronds used for thatching, stems for fibers; widely favored as ornamental plants

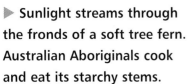

▶ Sunlight streams through the fronds of a soft tree fern. Australian Aboriginals cook and eat its starchy stems.

▼ Fiddleheads of the male fern. The tightly coiled heads and a dense coat of scales help protect the delicate growing tips of the ferns from damage.

See Also | BULBS, CORMS, & RHIZOMES **1** 34 | LEAVES **1** 38 | GROWING BIGGER **1** 46 👁

▲ ▶ **Extremes of fern form. Small pink fronds of the mosquito fern, *Azolla* (above), nestle among even tinier duckweeds, while the huge Tasmanian tree fern (right) has a trunk made up mainly of dead leaf-stalks.**

◀ **Fronds of the bird's nest fern are not divided into separate leaflets. The way they unfurl reveals their status as ferns.**

purple stems. Their stems or lower surfaces may be covered in scales or woolly outgrowths ranging from a brown color, through silvery tan, to bright yellow.

Special hairs on fern fronds may give off a scent when the leaf is crushed. North America has several hay-scented ferns, while

▲ Filmy ferns have very delicate fronds and live only in wet places.

◀ Typical fern fronds, with each leaf divided into pinnae and the pinnae into pinnules. Many ferns grow in shady, damp places in woodlands in North America.

some South American elephant ferns smell of citrus fruit. But not all ferns have pleasant smells; some maidenhair ferns smell like tomcats' urine!

Clumps and Colonies

Ferns can multiply in many different ways. Buds on the underground rhizomes send up new shoots at intervals. If the rhizome breaks up, the fragments simply put down adventitious roots and become independent plants, so you get clumps of ferns. In the sword ferns and some others, special side branches of the rhizome—stolons—grow back up toward the soil surface and produce new plants. In some ferns the leaf stalk grows beyond the final leaflet and arches down to touch the soil, where it forms a new plant with its own roots.

In some species little plantlets, or bulbils, grow on the fronds. They are identical to the parent plant; that is, they are clones. They develop roots; and if the frond finally curves down to touch the ground or is trampled on and rots away, they will take root. Bulbils without roots are sometimes used to survive harsh conditions. They drop off when mature and can stay dormant (resting) for several months.

Many ferns can also make new plants from buds on the gametophyte plant. The gametophytes of filmy ferns make gemmae, which can produce new gametophytes.

See Also | CELL TYPES & TISSUES *1* 18 | VEGETATIVE REPRODUCTION *2* 46 👁

Water Ferns

Many aquatic ferns spread rapidly by simply breaking up: each fragment becomes a new plant. The mosquito ferns (*Azolla*) of the tropics have tiny leaves only about 0.08 inches (2 mm) long. Air trapped between the overlapping leaves and the stem helps keep them afloat. *Azolla* is very special: its leaves contain nitrogen-fixing cyanobacteria. These ferns are often plowed back into the soil when a rice crop is harvested to replenish it with nitrates.

The leaves of water spangles (*Salvinia*) have hairs on their upper surface to trap air. These plants are popular in aquariums and garden pools but can cause havoc in the wild. Spreading fast across lakes and reservoirs, they cut off the oxygen supply to the underwater life and destroy local fishing industries. They also make waterways impassable to boats.

The water sprite of Asia is rooted in the mud, but its spongy leaf-stalks contain air, so the leaves rise to the surface. Water clovers have unusual leaves, like four-leaved clovers. As rain fills the pools, the leaf stalks grow quickly to keep the leaves at the surface.

Fertile Fronds Are Different

The principal way in which ferns reproduce is by generating spores that germinate to produce the sexual or gametophyte stage of the life cycle (see Life Cycle diagram below). The spore sacs of ferns develop directly on the leaves. Some species have separate fronds for making spores (fertile fronds). The moonworts are an example. The parsley fern usually has spreading, highly divided fronds with delicate stalks, but the fertile fronds are upright and undivided.

The osmundas, or flowering ferns, have yet another arrangement. The royal fern has fertile tips to its fronds, which are like light-brown flower heads. The interrupted fern produces fertile leaflets in the middle of its fronds: four pairs of dark green leaflets bear spore sacs that turn dark brown. The cinnamon fern,

LIFE CYCLE OF FERNS

The fern usually seen (1) is the sporophyte generation—each cell has two sets of chromosomes. This plant produces spores by meiosis, so that each contains only one set of chromosomes. Spores develop within little spore sacs (sporangia; 2) in clusters (sori) on the undersides of the fronds (3).

Each sporangium has a band of cells with thick inner and thin outer walls called an annulus. When a sporangium is ripe, it dries out. The outer walls of the annulus shrink, ripping open the sporangium in an area of weak cells (the stomium). This releases the tension in the annulus cells, and it snaps back into place, catapulting the spores out (4). This strategy ensures that the spores are released only in dry weather.

Spores germinate (5) to form a tiny, heart-shaped plate of cells

▼ An umbrellalike indusium protects sori of the male fern.

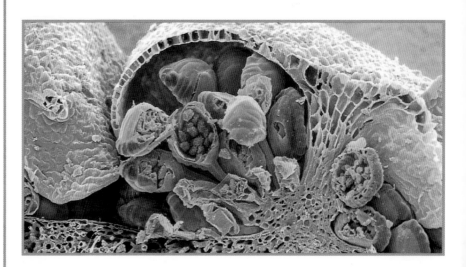

another osmunda, produces fertile fronds before the main fronds. They are stiff, club-shaped fronds divided into pairs of club-shaped spore-bearing leaflets close to the stem. By contrast, the sterile

▶ In moonworts fertile fronds (in the foreground) are distinct from the leafy fronds behind.

fronds are graceful, arching leaves.

Ferns can be difficult to identify by their leaves, since the differences between some of them are very small. But the way the spore sacs are arranged on the fertile fronds provides another clue to the species. The spores are produced in little spore sacs called sporangia. In some species

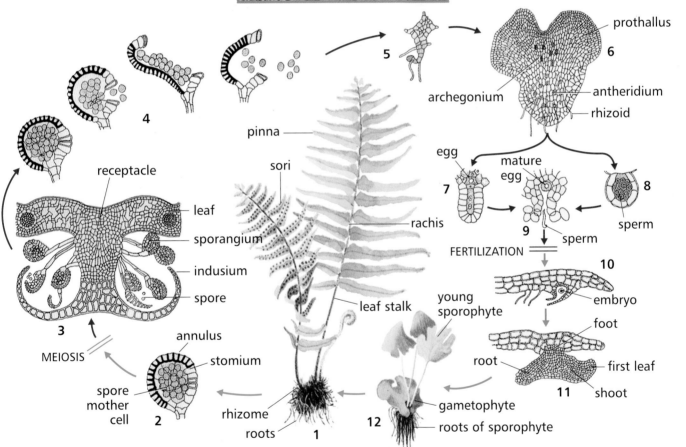

(prothallus; 6)—the gametophyte generation. At the top of the heart is a cushion of cells. The archegonia (7), which produce the egg cells, develop here. The antheridia (8) produce little male cells (sperm), which have tiny

whiplike hairs (undulipodia) that help them swim.

The prothallus grows close to the ground, trapping moisture for the sperm to swim in. Lured by chemicals made in the archegonia, they fertilize the eggs (9).

The embryo (10) grows a foot into the prothallus (11), absorbing nutrients from it. Then it grows its first leaf and a little rhizome (12), and soon begins to photosynthesize and become independent.

See Also | *NUTRITION 3 30* | *NITROGEN FIXATION 3 34* | *EVOLUTION OF PLANTS 6 4* 👁

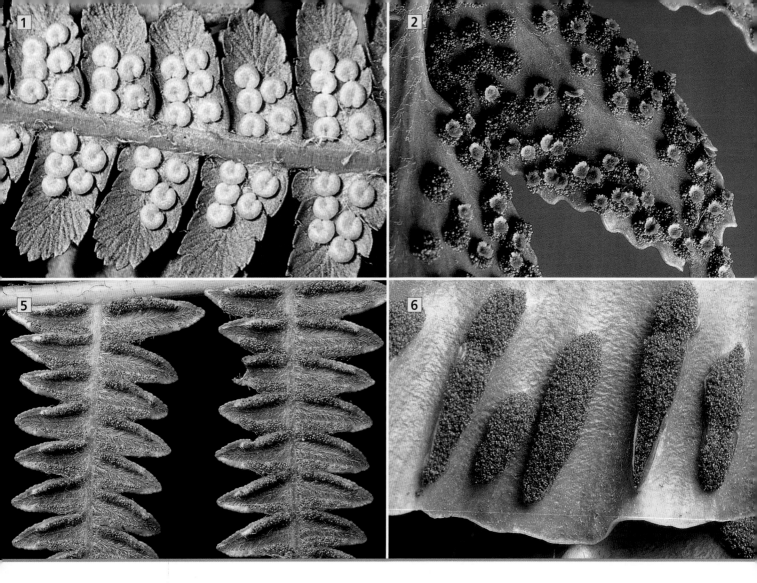

▲ The structure and arrangement of sori. They are often covered by a protective structure, the indusium, which may be kidney-shaped, as in this male fern (1), but shrivel when the sori are mature (2). Other arrangements are the maidenhair fern (3) with heart-shaped indusia; polypody (4) with rounded sori; bracken (5) with no indusia but inrolled leaf edges; hart's-tongue fern (6) with long, thin sori and indusia; staghorn fern (7) with the frond covered in sporangia; and spleenwort (8), with narrow indusia on the leaf edge.

the sporangia form clusters called sori. An umbrella-shaped flap of tissue called an indusium may cover the sori. In other species the sori are borne naked on the leaf or are covered by the edge of the frond, which curls inward to protect them.

Ferns of the Jungle

Tropical jungles provide ideal habitats for many ferns. Some live on the forest floor. Others live high up on the branches of the rainforest trees (these ferns are called epiphytes, from the Greek words *epi*, meaning "on," and *phuton*, meaning "plant"). A few are climbers, with their roots in the forest floor, and their fronds on the topmost branches hundreds of feet above, where their wind-blown spores can travel for miles. They may have twining stems or use suckerlike adventitious roots to cling to their hosts.

Many ferns, such as polypodies, grow on trees, anchored in the debris that collects in the crevices of the bark. Rain trickling down the tree picks up nutrients, and moist air rising from the forest floor stops the fronds from drying out. Bracket ferns boost their food

supply by keeping the bases of their fronds after they have died. They form a bracket that traps the remains of the dead leaves. The leaves rot, forming a rich compost into which the roots grow. Other plants—ribbon ferns, club mosses, and orchids—soon take root, and a hanging garden grows. The dead leaf bases of tree ferns also provide homes for epiphytes.

The potato fern and some polypodies have a novel way of getting food. The older, hollow rhizomes of these plants become home to colonies of ants. The ants both provide the fern with nutrients from their droppings and also guard the fronds against attack by other insects.

Some epiphytes are very large. The fronds of elephant's tongues may be several meters long, while the bird's nest fern can weigh over 220 pounds (100 kg). The bird's nest fern uses heavily branched roots to trap water like a sponge.

Tough Survivors

Ferns have also evolved ingenious ways of coping with dry conditions. They grow in deserts and in cracks and crevices on rocky cliffs where little rain falls. Their fronds may be covered in scales or hairs to reduce transpiration. Tight clusters of fronds that curl in dry weather can also trap air and reduce water loss. The European rustyback fern, which lives on limestone, can even survive losing 95 percent of its water content. Gold-back and silver-back ferns are among the first plants to take root on lava flows and on land ravaged by fire.

Some ferns, such as the resurrection ferns of Mexico, Africa, and Australia, dry up in droughts. The buds of the new fronds are protected from drying out by the

See Also | SURVIVING EXTREMES **3** 42 | COMPETITION **4** 28 | THE WORLD'S BIOMES **4** 36 ◉

remains of the dead ones. Resting buds develop into new fronds when rain returns. Some species, like the bead fern of the United States, may appear dry and dead, but when wetted, the frond quickly becomes green again.

From Food to Fibers

Ferns are important sources of food and medicines. The ostrich fern is sold as a delicacy in the United States, and tender young fiddleheads are eaten as a spring vegetable, rather like asparagus. The rhizomes and trunks of many species are a source of starch, which is usually roasted. Potato ferns are cultivated by the Maoris of New Zealand and buckler ferns by Native Americans and Inuit

DANGEROUS BRACKEN

Bracken (brake) is a large fern, up to 16 feet (5 m) tall, widespread throughout the world. Its creeping rhizomes spread rapidly, so that it covers vast areas of poor soils and wasteland. Besides being a troublesome weed, its young fronds contain cyanide, probably to put off leaf-eating insects. Bracken is poisonous to cattle and horses, and can cause blindness. Its tissues contain chemicals that can cause cancer in humans and other animals—and so do its spores. It is unwise to walk through bracken that is shedding its spores.

◀ Many fern species are cultivated as houseplants, and different varieties have been bred. Shown here is an erect sword fern.

▶ The elkhorn fern is an epiphyte—in other words, it grows on the branches of trees and gets all its nutrients from rainwater trickling down the tree trunk. The large upright leaves are its fertile fronds.

peoples. The fruiting bodies of a water fern, nardoo, are made into cakes by Australian Aboriginals. Bread is made from bracken rhizomes in many parts of the world, and the fronds of some fern species are boiled in water to make tea.

Many folk medicines and herbal remedies use ferns as a key ingredient. The maidenhair fern, a popular houseplant, is used to treat a variety of illnesses, from asthma and smallpox to snake bites, as well as diseases of many internal organs and even insanity!

Spleenworts are named for their shape, which resembles a spleen, and are used to treat enlarged spleens. Male ferns were used in medieval love potions and, until recently, in expensive perfumes. The fiddleheads of male fern were thought to protect people against evil spirits. Poultices made from ferns are used to treat wounds, burns, and ulcers. Bracken fiddleheads help soothe insect bites.

Fibers from fern fronds can be used as twine, and the stems of scrambling ferns are made into ropes, baskets, and fish traps. Fern stems and fronds are a source of dyes. Large fronds provide thatch for roofs and bedding for livestock. Tree fern trunks are a good source of timber. The wiry roots of some osmundas hold moisture and are often used as bases for growing epiphytic orchids.

Ferns are much prized for their decorative beauty. The Christmas fern is a popular table decoration in North America. In artificial settings, such as floral arrangements or gardens, the great variety of shapes, sizes, and colors of ferns really comes into its own.

Cycads CYCADOPHYTA

RELICS OF A GLORIOUS PAST, cycads look like a cross between a palm tree and a conifer. They have thick stems, whorls of palmlike or fernlike leaves, and large cones. Over 200 million years ago cycads dominated the landscape. Today, many species are endangered by overcollecting for gardens and by loss of habitat.

Cycads are slow-growing and long-lived—some may even be 1,000 years old. They range from small shrubs such as *Zamia*, found in the United States, to palmlike trees over 60 feet (18 m) tall. Their unbranched stems are the same thickness from top to bottom. They do not have much woody tissue, but the hard overlapping bases of old leaves help support them. Some low-growing cycads have tuberlike underground stems.

Most cycads have huge taproots up to 40 feet (12 m) long. They also produce unusual roots that are shaped like branching corals (coralloid roots). These roots grow back up toward the surface of the soil. They contain fungi and bacteria. The fungi help the cycad take up nutrients, while the bacteria fix nitrogen from the soil atmosphere into nitrates that the cycads can use.

Record-breakers

Cycads produce cones, not flowers. Male and female cones are produced on separate plants.

The female cones are shorter and fatter than the male cones, and can weigh as much as 100 pounds (45 kg). No other plant produces such large cones. As in conifers, the ovules contain archegonia. They, in turn, contain the largest egg cells in the plant kingdom, up to 0.25 inches (3 mm) across—large enough to see with the naked eye.

The male cones are quite large, too, some 20 inches (50 cm) long. They release massive quantities of pollen: a single male cone of *Encephalartos* can produce 7 billion pollen grains. Both wind

and insects help disperse cycad pollen. The male cones of some species generate a lot of heat—they may be 27°F (15°C) warmer than their surroundings. In some cycads both male and female cones give off a musty odor that also attracts insects. The warmth and odor both attract insects like beetles.

When a cycad pollen grain germinates, it grows a pollen tube into the ovule. The two sperm that are released by the pollen tube are the largest in the entire plant kingdom, measuring up to 0.02 inches (0.5 mm) in diameter,

---

CYCADS

Phylum:
  Cycadophyta

NUMBER OF GENERA: 11

NUMBER OF SPECIES:
  145–200

DISTRIBUTION: tropical and
  subtropical regions, notably Indonesia, Malaysia, southern Africa,
  South America, and Australia

ECONOMIC USES: starch from the sago cycad (*Cycas revoluta*) is eaten;
  leaves used as roofing; ground seeds and buds used as dressings

▲ The female cone of the sago cycad is one of the largest cones in the world.

◀ The treelike cycad *Encephalartos caffer* grows in the mountains of South Africa. Starch from its stems is used to make a traditional staple food called kaffir bread.

with about 40,000 undulipodia (whiplike hairs for swimming). They swim through a fluid-filled chamber to reach the eggs.

Like many flowering plants, cycad seeds store food in two fleshy seed leaves (cotyledons). These seeds have a fleshy, brightly colored outer coat that is rich in starch and attracts a wide range of birds and mammals, from pigeons to elephants. A few species use water for seed dispersal.

Cooking Cycads

Cycads are an important source of food. The most significant staple foodstuff that they yield is starch, which comes from their trunks. This product is sometimes called sago; care is needed in its preparation, since it is poisonous in its raw state and must be cooked in a special way to make it safe. Roasted cycad seeds are also eaten in many countries.

Dried cycad leaves are used in decorations and for thatching roofs. Cut cycad stems release a sticky gum, which is used as an adhesive. Ground seeds and crushed buds make effective dressings for wounds and ulcers.

See Also | *NITROGEN FIXATION* **3** *34* | *WHAT IS A CONIFER?* **8** *4* | *PALM FAMILY* **9** *30* ◉

Welwitschia and Allies GNETOPHYTA

A 2,000-YEAR-OLD PLANT with just two huge leaves up to 20 feet (6 m) long, *Welwitschia* is a very strange organism indeed. This tough plant grows only in the Namib Desert on the southwest coast of Africa.

Welwitschia is unlike any other plant on Earth. It is basically a squat, woody stem about 2 feet (60 cm) across, which produces just two straplike leaves up to 6 feet (1.8 m) wide. They grow from their bases throughout the plant's life. The leaves lie on the sand, and their tips become tattered with age into leathery strips. *Welwitschia* absorbs moisture from the sea fogs that often roll across its coastal desert habitat.

Surprisingly for a desert plant, its air pores (stomata) stay open all day, so they lose a lot of water. The high rates of transpiration probably cool the plant. *Welwitschia* also has a taproot, which may reach underground water sources.

A Strange Combination

Like conifers, *Welwitschia* produces reddish male and female cones. The female cones bear ovules rather like those of flowering plants. Ovules develop to contain the eggs.

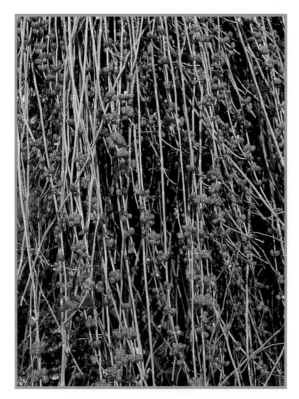

The male cones produce pollen grains, which grow a pollen tube to carry the male nuclei to the egg cells. *Welwitschia* has a kind of double fertilization rather like that of flowering plants, but not exactly the same. The fertilized ovule ripens into a seed and stores food in two seed leaves (cotyledons) in the embryo. The outer covering of the ovule forms a wing, and the seeds are carried away by the wind.

▶ **Welwitschia grows in the deserts of southern Africa. Its short stem bears two large, tattered leaves.**

◀ **The fruits of a joint fir from Greece. Scalelike structures (bracts) from the female cone become swollen and juicy, like a berry.**

Joint Firs

Welwitschia is related to the joint firs, or ephedras—shrubs, climbers, and small trees that live in dry places. Ephedras have tiny, scalelike leaves and green, jointed stems that photosynthesize. The female cones produce ovules with archegonia that contain the eggs, like those of conifers. The male flower has a single stamen.

Some joint fir species called *Ma-huang* produce ephedrine, which is used in Chinese medicine to treat ulcers and to help cold sufferers sweat and breathe more easily. Extracts of the stems are used to make Mormon tea, Mexican tea, squaw tea, and desert tea.

Ancient Origins

These plants have many features in common with flowering plants. Their wood contains true xylem vessels. The leaves of some species (*Gnetum*) have a netlike pattern of veins. The seeds have two cotyledons holding stored food and are dispersed in a fruitlike structure.

Fossils suggest that *Welwitschia* evolved over 300 million years ago from ancient plants that were also the ancestors of modern conifers.

GNETOPHYTES

Phylum:
  Gnetophyta

NUMBER OF GENERA: 4

NUMBER OF SPECIES: 95

DISTRIBUTION: *Welwitschia*:
  southwestern Africa;
  Gnetum: tropics; *Ephedra*: mainly worldwide

ECONOMIC USES: original source of ephedrine (now made synthetically), used as a decongestant to treat such conditions as asthma and sinusitis

---

See Also | FERTILIZATION **2** 26 | WHAT IS A CONIFER? **8** 4 | WHAT IS A FLOWERING PLANT? **9** 4

Ginkgo GINKGOPHYTA

A SURVIVOR FROM THE AGE OF THE DINOSAURS, the ginkgo is the oldest living plant species. It arose some 350 million years ago, and fossilized ginkgoes 20 million years old still survive in the Ginkgo Petrified Forest State Park in Washington State.

When ginkgoes first appeared, South America was still joined to Africa, and it was easy for trees to spread around the world. But many were killed off by the last Ice Age. Just a few survived in the mountains of China, where they have been planted in temples for thousands of years.

The tree gets its name from the Japanese word *ginkyo*, which means "silver apricot." Its fruits are, indeed, silvery, and the seeds are edible. The Chinese eat them roasted, rather like we eat peanuts. When the ginkgo first arrived in the West (in England), it was given the name "maidenhair tree" because its leaves looked like those of the maidenhair fern.

An Elegant Tree

The ginkgo has a slim trunk and graceful, curving branches. The leaves are fan-shaped with wavy edges. They grow in clusters on short shoots. Their veins fork in two over and over again. The bark is rough, with strange breastlike knobs called "chi-chis."

Male and female flowers are produced on separate trees.

▲ In the fall ginkgo leaves put on a spectacular display, turning from a dull, pale green to this striking, butter-yellow color.

▼ The male flowers of the ginkgo tree are simply catkinlike cones of stamens.

pair of ovules will develop after fertilization. It grows into a fruit like a small, silvery-green plum.

Long on Memory

Ginkgo is a popular plant in alternative medicine, especially as an aid to short-term memory and to slow down aging. It can also help patients with Alzheimer's disease. The Chinese have used it for thousands of years as a remedy to help them enjoy a long life.

The ginkgo is planted in parks and on sidewalks the world over. Ginkgoes evolved even earlier than leaf-eating insects and so are hardly affected by them. They are not much affected by pollution or diseases, either, and thrive beside the busiest city streets—even on Fifth Avenue, New York. Maybe this resilience is the secret of its long life—some ginkgoes are at least 1,000 years old.

Female trees do not produce true flowers, but simply have pairs of ovules (which contain the eggs) on long stalks. The male trees produce catkins full of stamens. When the pollen germinates, it releases swimming male sperm instead of the pollen tubes in flowering plants. Only one of each

◀ The ginkgo (left) is a tall, elegant tree that grows up to 125 feet (38 m). This example is in Central Park, New York City.

GINKGO

Phylum:
  Ginkgophyta

NUMBER OF GENERA: 1

NUMBER OF SPECIES: 1

DISTRIBUTION: almost extinct in the wild, surviving only in China. Planted as an ornamental in North America and Europe

ECONOMIC USES: in traditional Chinese herbal medicine extracts from the ginkgo tree are used to aid short-term memory and to delay the aging process

See Also | WHAT IS A CONIFER? **8** 4 | WHAT IS A FLOWERING PLANT? **9** 4

Glossary

adventitious root A root that grows in an unusual position or from an unusual part of the plant.

alternation of generations A life cycle in which HAPLOID and DIPLOID organisms alternate.

antheridium An organ producing male SEX CELLS.

archegonium (*pl.* **archegonia**) An organ producing female SEX CELLS.

asexual reproduction A form of reproduction that produces genetically identical offspring; it does not involve the fusing of male and female SEX CELLS—only one parent is required.

bacterium (*pl.* **bacteria**) Microscopic organism that lacks a true cell nucleus. Most are single-celled.

bulbil A small bulb that grows from an aerial bud that develops above ground. A bulbil is easily detached, and a new plant can be grown from it. "Cloves" of garlic are bulbils.

capsule A dry FRUIT that splits open to release its SEEDS. In MOSSES it is a tough-walled container in which asexual SPORES are produced. Also, a layer of mucilage coating the cell walls of some BACTERIA.

carbohydrate A simple sugar or a molecule made up of sugar units.

carnivorous plant A plant that supplements its nitrogen supply by trapping insects and other small animals. The plant may secrete digestive juices to convert the nitrogen compounds into a form it can absorb, or it may rely on BACTERIA to do the job for it.

chloroplast A small membrane-bounded "bag," or organelle, that is the site of PHOTOSYNTHESIS in the cells of plants and algae. It contains membranes covered in chlorophyll.

chromosome A structure that contains genetic information. Shaped like a thread, it is made from a complex arrangement of proteins and DNA.

club moss Evergreen VASCULAR PLANT of the phylum Lycophyta. Club mosses have small leaves arranged spirally around the stem. They produce little cones of tiny leaves bearing SPORE sacs.

companion cell A cell that lies adjacent to a PHLOEM SIEVE TUBE and is thought to supply it with energy.

conducting tissue Tissues that conduct water or food through a plant or alga.

cone A group of closely packed, modified leaves surrounding a central axis that bears the reproductive structures of a plant.

conifer A tree that bears its seeds in CONES. Conifers are classed in the phylum Coniferophyta, which includes pines, firs, spruces, hemlocks, Douglas firs, junipers, and yews.

cortex The outer part of an organ, for example, of the stem.

cotyledon (seed leaf) The first leaf or leaves of a plant EMBRYO. The SEED contains one or more cotyledons. After GERMINATION, PHOTOSYNTHESIS in the cotyledons sustains the plant until its true leaves appear.

cuticle The waxy layer that coats the body of a plant to reduce water loss. It is deposited on the outer surface of the EPIDERMAL cell walls.

Cyanobacteria A large and varied group (phylum) of BACTERIA that contain chlorophyll and are able to PHOTOSYNTHESIZE. They were formerly known as blue-green algae.

cycad A CONE-bearing plant of the phylum Cycadophyta. Male and female cones are borne on separate plants. Although they resemble palms, cycads are not related to them; they evolved millions of years earlier.

diploid Having cells with two sets of CHROMOSOMES.

dormancy (*adj.* **dormant**) A state in which—as a result of hormone action—growth is suspended and metabolic activity is reduced to a minimum.

double fertilization In flowering plants the fusion of one male nucleus with the egg nucleus to produce a ZYGOTE and the simultaneous fusion of a second male nucleus with two other female nuclei to create the endosperm tissue.

elaters Elongated filaments that disperse spores.

embryo A young plant, after fertilization has occurred, when the cells have started to differentiate into particular structures.

epidermis (*adj.* **epidermal**) The outermost layer of cells of a plant body.

epiphyte A plant that grows on the surface of another plant, but does not take nutrients from it.

fern A plant that has spirally arranged megaphylls (large leaves with several veins). It produces SPORES, and sperm with many UNDULIPODIA.

fruit In flowering plants a mature,

ripe ovary, or group of ovaries, containing the seeds.

fungus (*pl.* **fungi**) An organism that lacks chlorophyll and so does not PHOTOSYNTHESIZE. Fungi produce spores and do not have UNDULIPODIA at any stage of their life. Although they resemble plants superficially, they are a distinct kingdom, the Fungi.

gamete (sex cell) HAPLOID cell that fuses with a haploid cell from another individual of opposite sex or mating type to form a DIPLOID ZYGOTE that will develop into a new individual.

gametophyte The structure in which the HAPLOID reproductive cells are produced. It is the haploid generation in the life cycle of the plant.

gemma (*pl.* **gemmae**) A small, plate-like cluster of cells produced by a MOSS or LIVERWORT. It can grow into an independent new plant identical to its parent.

germination The moment when a growing plant EMBRYO breaks through the seed coat (testa).

ginkgo The only living species of the phylum Gingkophyta that produces catkins of pollen-bearing male flowers and fleshy OVULES on a long stalk. The leaf veins repeatedly branch in two. The seeds are fleshy, with a stony center. The sperm have spiral bands of UNDULIPODIA.

haploid Having only one copy of each CHROMOSOME in every cell.

hornwort Nonvascular plant of the phylum Anthocerophyta. Hornworts are similar to LIVERWORTS, but have long, cylindrical SPOROPHYTES, ELATERS to disperse the SPORES, and cells containing a single large CHLOROPLAST containing a pyrenoid (a small protein granule). The spores germinate directly into young GAMETOPHYTES.

horsetail VASCULAR PLANT of the phylum Sphenophyta. Horsetails have jointed stems with whorls of SCALE LEAVES and green PHOTOSYNTHETIC branches at each joint. The SPORANGIA are borne in cones.

integument A protective layer of tissue that surrounds an OVULE completely, except for the MICROPYLE.

liverwort Nonvascular plant of the phylum Hepatophyta. Many liverworts have flattened bodies; leafy species have three rows of leaflike lobes. The SPORE CAPSULE splits into four valves. The spores are dispersed with the aid of ELATERS.

megasporangium A SPORANGIUM that produces HAPLOID female SPORES (MEGASPORES). In seed-producing plants the OVULE is a megasporangium.

megaspore A HAPLOID structure that develops into a female GAMETOPHYTE.

meiosis (reduction division) Form of nuclear division in which nuclei divide twice to produce four HAPLOID nuclei, each having half the number of CHROMOSOMES of the parent nucleus.

micropyle The small opening at the tip of an OVULE through which pollen enters the NUCELLUS.

microsporangium The structure that produces HAPLOID MICROSPORES (POLLEN GRAINS). In seed-producing plants the pollen grain is the microsporangium.

microspore A HAPLOID SPORE that develops into a male GAMETOPHYTE.

moss A small plant whose main generation is HAPLOID (the GAMETOPHYTE) and consists of a stem with spirally arranged leaves, anchored by multicellular RHIZOIDS. The male

and female SEX CELLS meet in the ARCHEGONIA, and the new DIPLOID SPOROPHYTE generation grows on the GAMETOPHYTE, producing a SPORE CAPSULE on a long stalk. The spores, dispersed with the aid of ELATERS, GERMINATE to form branched threads called PROTONEMATA, from which new plants arise.

nitrogen fixation The incorporation of molecules of nitrogen gas into compounds that can be absorbed by plants.

nucellus A mass of unspecialized cells in the OVULE. It contains the embryo sac and egg cell.

ovule The structure inside the ovary that contains the egg cell inside an embryo sac, with the tissues that nourish it. After fertilization the ovule will develop into a SEED.

phloem Tissue composed of tubular cells, arranged end to end, through which sugars are transported from the leaves to every other part of the plant.

photosynthesis The process by which green plants manufacture sugar from carbon dioxide and water, using sunlight energy.

pigment A chemical that reflects certain colors of light, so appearing colored; for example, chlorophyll.

pollen grain A small structure that contains HAPLOID male nuclei.

pollen tube The tube by which the male nuclei travel from the POLLEN GRAIN, through the stigma and style, and into the OVULE for fertilization.

protonema (*pl.* **protonemata**) Juvenile form of a MOSS or LIVERWORT. In mosses it is usually thread-like, but in some liverworts it is a delicate plate of cells. Adult plants develop from buds on the protonema.

rhizoid Delicate hairlike structures that anchor MOSSES, LIVERWORTS, and some molds and algae to surfaces. In mosses they are multicellular.

rhizome An underground stem that grows horizontally. It has branches and new stems grow vertically upward from points along it, so it allows the plant to spread.

root The underground part of the main axis of a VASCULAR PLANT, specialized for anchorage, absorption of water and minerals, and sometimes also food or water storage. Vascular tissues form a central core (stele). Root hairs are produced just behind the root tip. Branch roots arise from deep inside the root.

sclerenchyma Supporting tissue in which the walls of many cells are heavily thickened with lignin.

seed The dispersal structure that develops from a fertilized OVULE. It contains a single plant EMBRYO and a food supply, which may be in the form of endosperm or swollen COTYLEDONS, surrounded by a seed coat (testa).

seed leaf *See* COTYLEDONS.

sex cell *See* GAMETES.

sexual reproduction Reproduction that involves the fusing of male and female GAMETES. The offspring contain genes from both parents and are not identical to either.

sieve tube PHLOEM cell with perforated end walls that allow transport of sugars and other substances up and down the plant.

species A group of organisms that can breed among themselves but not with other organisms.

sporangiophore A structure bearing one or more SPORANGIA.

sporangium (*pl.* **sporangia**) A structure in which SPORES are formed.

spore A reproductive cell that can develop into an adult without needing to fuse with another cell.

sporophyll A modified leaf or leaflike organ that bears SPORANGIA. For example, the fertile fronds of ferns and the STAMEN and carpels of flowering plants are sporophylls.

sporophyte A plant during the generation in its life cycle when its cells are DIPLOID.

stamen The male reproductive organ in a flower, consisting of an anther borne on a filament.

starch The principal form in which plants store nutrients. It is made during PHOTOSYNTHESIS. Starch is readily converted to sugars by enzymes known as amylases.

stomata (*sing.* **stoma**) Pores in the surface of leaves (and sometimes also stems) through which gas exchange takes place. Carbon dioxide for PHOTOSYNTHESIS and oxygen for respiration enter the plant, and water vapor, carbon dioxide, and oxygen leave it.

strobilus A number of SPORE-bearing leaves (SPOROPHYLLS), or OVULE-bearing scales, grouped around a central axis. Also called a CONE.

symbiosis (*adj.* **symbiotic**) A close relationship between members of two different species from which both partners benefit.

thallus (*pl.* **thalli**) A plant body that is not divided into leaf, stem, and root.

tracheid A type of cell found in XYLEM tissue in VASCULAR PLANTS other than flowering plants. Long, narrow, and with tapering ends, adjacent tracheids overlap. There are

perforations, mainly in the end walls, through which water can flow.

transpiration The loss of water from a plant by evaporation, mainly through its STOMATA.

tube cell In POLLEN GRAINS the cell that develops into the POLLEN TUBE, but disappears after fertilization.

undulipodium (*pl.* **undulipodia**) A microscopic, whiplike structure used to propel single-celled eukaryotic organisms, including sperm, through the water.

vascular bundle A strand of tissue made up of the cells through which water, nutrients, and sugar are transported through the plant. It usually contains XYLEM and PHLOEM.

vascular plant A plant that has XYLEM and PHLOEM.

vegetative shoot A strand of tissue through which water, nutrients, and sugar are carried through the plant. It contains XYLEM and PHLOEM.

vein Bundle of XYLEM and PHLOEM.

vessel Name given to tubelike cells in XYLEM and PHLOEM.

whisk fern VASCULAR PLANT of the phylum Psilophyta. They have stems that repeatedly fork in two, minute leaflike structures, and RHIZOIDS rather than ROOTS. Their vascular tissue consists of TRACHEIDS and poorly defined PHLOEM.

xylem Tissue composed of tubular cells arranged end to end, through which water and dissolved nutrients are transported from the roots to every other part of the plant.

zygote The cell that is formed by the fusion of the male and female reproductive cells (GAMETES) before it has undergone division.

Scientific Names

In this set common names have been used wherever possible. Listed below are the plants mentioned in this volume for which scientific names have not already been given. See Volume 1, page 7 for further detail on the naming of plants.

Aglaophyton *Aglaophyton*

Asteroxylon *Asteroxylon*

bead fern *Cheilanthes covillei*

bird's nest fern *Asplenium nidus*

bog mosses *Sphagnum* species

bracken *Pteridium aquilinum*

brake *Pteridium aquilinum*

buckler ferns *Dryopteris* species

calamites *Calamites* species

chain ferns *Woodwardia* species

Christmas fern *Polystichum acrostichoides*

cinnamon fern *Osmunda cinnamomea*

cliffbrakes *Pellaea* species

club mosses *Lycopodium* species; also phylum Lycophyta

common horsetail *Equisetum arvense*

common scouring rush *Equisetum hyemale*

conifers: phylum Coniferophyta

cord moss *Funaria hygrometrica*

Cryptothallus *Cryptothallus* species

cycads: phylum Cycadophyta

duckweeds *Lemna* species

electric fern *Selaginella willdenovii*

elephant ferns *Angiopteris* species

elephant's tongues *Elaphoglossum* species

elkhorn fern *Platycerium bifurcatum*

Encephalartos *Encephalartos* species

ephedras *Ephedra* species

ferns: phylum Filicinophyta

field horsetail *Equisetum arvense*

filmy ferns: family Hymenophyllaceae

fir club moss *Lycopodium selago*

floury cloak fern *Cheilanthes farinosa*

fragrant fern *Microsorum scandens*

fringe mosses *Grimmia* species

Frullania *Frullania* species

giant horsetail (S.Am.) *Equisetum giganteum*; (USA) *Equisetum praealtum*

ginkgo *Ginkgo biloba*

gnetums *Gnetum* species

gold back fern *Pityrogramma triangularis*

granite mosses *Andreaea* species

great horsetail *Equisetum telmateia*

ground cedar *Lycopodium complanatum, L. tristachyum*

ground pines *Lycopodium* species in general, *L. obscurum* and *L. tristachyum* in particular

hair-cap mosses *Polytrichum* species

hart's-tongue fern *Phyllitis scolopendrium*

hayscented fern *Dennstaedtia punctilobula*

holly fern *Polystichum braunii*

Horneophyton *Horneophyton* species

hornworts: phylum Anthocerophyta

horsetails *Equisetum* species; also phylum Sphenophyta

interrupted fern *Osmunda claytoniana*

Irish moss *Chondrus* species

Japanese painted fern *Athyrium niponicum*

joint firs *Ephedra* species

Lepidodendron *Lepidodendron* species

liverworts: phylum Hepatophyta

Lunularia *Lunularia* species

maidenhair ferns *Adiantum* species

maidenhair tree *Ginkgo biloba*

male fern *Dryopteris felix-mas*

marchantias *Marchantia* species

moonworts *Botrychium* species

mosquito ferns *Azolla* species

mosses: phylum Bryophyta

nardoo *Marsilea drummondii*

orchids: family Orchidaceae

osmundas *Osmunda* species

ostrich fern *Matteucia struthiopteris*

parsley fern *Cryptogramma crispa*

peat mosses *Sphagnum* species

Pellia *Pellia* species

Peltigera *Peltigera* species

phylloglossum *Phylloglossum drummondii*

pigeon wheats *Polytrichum* species

polypody *Polypodium* species

Porella *Porella* species

potato ferns *Marattia salicina,*

Solanopteris brunei

Psaronius *Psaronius* species

Psilophyton *Psilophyton* species

quillwort *Isoetes* species

reindeer moss *Cladonia rangiferina, C. stellaris*

resurrection fern *Polypodium polypodioides*

resurrection plant *Selaginella lepidophylla*

ribbon fern *Ophioglossum pendulum*

Riccia *Riccia* species

rough horsetail *Equisetum hyemale*

royal fern *Osmunda regalis*

running pine *Lycopodium clavatum*

rustyback fern *Asplenium ceterach, Ceterach officinarum*

sago cycad *Cycas revoluta*

scouring rushes *Equisetum* species

screw mosses *Tortula* species

Sigillaria *Sigillaria* species

silver back ferns *Pityrogramma* species

Sphaerocarpus *Sphaerocarpus* species

spike-moss *Selaginella* species

Splachnum *Splachnum* species

spleenworts *Asplenium* species

staghorn club moss *Lycopodium clavatum*

staghorn fern *Platycerium andinum*

sword ferns *Nephrolepis* species

Tasmanian tree fern *Dicksonia antarctica*

Tortella *Tortella tortuosa*

twisted mosses *Tortula* species

water clover *Marsilea polycarpa*

water ferns *Azolla* species

water horsetail *Equisetum fluviatile*

water spangles *Salvinia molesta*

water sprite *Ceratopteris thalictroides*

Welwitschia *Welwitschia mirabilis*

whisk ferns: phylum Psilophyta

wood horsetail *Equisetum sylvaticum*

Zamia *Zamia* species

Zosterophyllum *Zosterophyllum* species

Set Index

Major entries are shown by bold key words with relevant page numbers underlined. **Bold** numbers indicate volumes. *Italic* numbers indicate picture captions.

Scientific names of plants cited under common names in this Index are to be found at the end of each individual volume.

genetic engineering *see* genetic modification
"jumping genes" **2**: 44–45
Law of Random Assortment **2**: 44
Law of Segregation **2**: 42
reactions to stimuli **3**: 18
genus **1**: 7, **10**: 4
geranium **1**: 40, **2**: *10, 38, 49*

germination
epigeal **1**: 44, *44*
hypogeal **1**: 44, *45*
pollen **2**: 26, *26*
seed **1**: 22–23, <u>44–45</u>, *44–45*, **2**: 28–30, *28, 29*, **8**: *7*, **9**: 6–7, *7, 8*
triggers **1**: 45, **2**: 30, **3**: 12, 14, 22–23, *22, 42*
Gethyllis **9**: 26
gherkin **5**: 22, 23, **10**: 18
Gibasis graminifolia **9**: 36, *37*
gibberellic acid **1**: 45, **3**: *13, 14*
gibberellin **3**: 14–16, *23*
gill **6**: 34, *34, 35*, 37, 40
ginger **5**: 38, *38*, 41, **9**: 10
ginkgo 1: *5*, **4**: 32, **6**: *4*, **7**: 18, <u>48–49</u>, *48, 49*
Ginkgophyta 7: <u>48–49</u>
gladiolus **2**: *10*, 15, 36, **9**: 28, *28*, 29, *29*
gland **1**: 18, *21*, **3**: 36, **10**: 34, 35, 36, 42
glasswort **3**: *46*
global climate and plants 4: <u>34–35</u>
global warming **7**: 19
globe artichoke **5**: 17, *19*, **10**: 46
globeflower **10**: *9*
glucose **3**: 6
gnetale **1**: *5*
Gnetophyta 7: <u>46–47</u>
gnetophyte **6**: *4*, 11
Gnetum **7**: 47
goat grass **5**: *6*
gold **7**: 31
Golgi apparatus **1**: *13, 14–15*, **6**: *8*
gonium **6**: *9*
gooseberry **2**: 32, 34, **5**: *8*
goosegrass **2**: *38*
gorse **2**: 39
gourd **5**: 23, **10**: 18
bottle *see* calabash
ivy **10**: *19*
snake **10**: *19*
gourd-tree **1**: 32
grafting **2**: 49, **3**: 23
gram **5**: 25, **10**: 30
Grammatophyllum speciosum **9**: 16
granadilla **4**: 40
grape **3**: 16, **4**: 28, **5**: 8, 41, *41*
grape hyacinth **9**: 20–21
grapefruit **5**: 8, 10, **10**: 36
grass 1: *22, 23*, 32, 40, 43, **2**: 24–25, *24*
domestication **5**: 4–6, *6*
family 9: <u>12–15</u>, *13, 14, 15*

marine **2**: 25
nastic movements **3**: 20–21
pollination **9**: 8
roots **1**: *22, 23, 23, 26*
vegetative reproduction **2**: 48, **9**: 12, 14
see also cereal
grassland **1**: 37, **4**: 34
temperate **4**: 36, 42–43, *42*
tropical **4**: 36, 42, 43
gravitropism **3**: *13*, 18, *18*, 20
gravity **1**: 24, 44, **3**: *13*, 18, *18*, 20
greenhouse effect **7**: 19
groundnut (peanut) **3**: *28*, **5**: *14, 24, 25*, 30, **10**: 30
groundsel **10**: 48
growth 1: 16, 22, <u>46–49</u>, *46–49*, **5**: 44, **6**: 8–9, 11
control **3**: 12–16, *13*
roots **1**: *24*, 25
triggers **1**: 34, **3**: 12, 33
tropisms **3**: 18–23, *18–23*
growth substances *see* hormone
guard cell **1**: *39*, **3**: *6*, 29
guava **5**: *10*
gurania **10**: *19*
guttation **3**: *28*, 29
gymnosperm **1**: *5*, **6**: *4*, 11
see also cone; conifer
gynoecium **2**: *6*, **9**: 6, *7*
Gynostemma pentaphyllum **10**: *19*

H

habitat **4**: 8
Haeckel, Ernst **4**: 4
hairs
leaves and stems **1**: 18, *19*, 43, **3**: 44, *44*, 49, **7**: 10, 27, 38, 41
Halicystis **1**: *15*
haploid **6**: 10, 21, 23, **7**: 6, 10
hardwood **1**: 48, **5**: 44, 46, **8**: *9*
harebell **10**: 44
hare's ear **6**: *46*
hat thrower **6**: 32
haustorium **3**: 40–41, *40*, **6**: 40
hawthorn **10**: 26
hazel **2**: 24, 35, 38, **5**: *14*
heartwood **1**: 48, **5**: 44
heat
conservation **3**: 20, 48–49, **7**: 27
generation **2**: 20, **7**: 44
heath **4**: 39
heather **4**: 39, **10**: 22, *23*
bell **10**: 22
Heliophila coronopifolia **10**: *21*
hellebore **2**: *10*, **10**: *9*, 10
helmet flower **10**: *9*
helvella, fluted white **6**: *46*
hemlock **4**: 31, **10**: 38
hemlock (conifer) **5**: 44, 46, **8**: *4*, <u>22–23</u>, *23*
Canada **8**: 22, *22*

Carolina **8**: 22
Chinese **8**: 22
Japanese **8**: 22
mountain **8**: 22
western **5**: 44, **8**: 22, *22*
hemp **2**: 18, **5**: 31, 35, *35*
Manila (abacá) **9**: 40
hemp dogbane **5**: 35
henbane **5**: 42
black **10**: 41
Hepatophyta 7: <u>4–7</u>
herb **1**: 46, **4**: 40, **5**: 36, *37*
herbaceous perennial **3**: 43
herbicide **4**: 30, 31
hesperidium **2**: *34*
heterobasidiomycetae **6**: 37
hibiscus **2**: 10, 23, 24
hilum **2**: 29
histone **1**: 16
hogweed **9**: *5*
giant **4**: 30
Holantarctic **4**: 35, *35*
Holarctic **4**: 35, *35*
holdfast **6**: 28, *28*
hollyhock **2**: *16*
homobasidiomycetae **6**: 37
homologous pair **2**: 41
honesty **10**: *20, 21*
honey mushroom **6**: 39
honeysuckle **1**: 33
hop **1**: 33, **5**: 41
hop tree **10**: 36
hormone 1: 34, 45, **2**: 30, 32, **3**: <u>12–17</u>, *12–17*, 19–20, 21, 23, 29, 42, **6**: 6, 33
as defence mechanism **4**: 31
hornbeam **2**: 36
hornwort **1**: *5*, **3**: *5*, **6**: *4*, **7**: 16, *16*
Horneophyton **7**: 18
horseradish **5**: 38, **10**: 20
horsetail **1**: *5*, **6**: *4*, 9, **7**: 18, 19, *21*, <u>28–33</u>
common **7**: 28, 30, 32, *32*
giant (great) **7**: 28, *29*, 32
life cycle **7**: 30, *30*
rough (common scouring rush) **7**: 32
South American giant **7**: 28
water **7**: *31, 32*
wood **7**: 32
horticulture 5: <u>48–49</u>
and conservation **5**: 48
light levels **3**: 23
see also cultivation
houseleek **2**: *48*
hummingbird **2**: 24
hyacinth **9**: 20
hydra **6**: 22
hydroid **7**: 8–9
hydrological cycle *see* water
hydrostatic skeleton **1**: 15
hydrotropism **3**: 19, *19*
hymenium **6**: 35, *35*, 39
hypha **6**: 17, 30, 31, 33, 34, *35*, 37, 39–41, *44*, 48, **9**: 16
hypocotyl **1**: *22*, 24, 44, *44*

hypogeal germination **1**: 44, *45*
hypogyny **2**: *7*, **9**: *5*
hyssop **5**: 37

I

IAA *see* indoleacetic acid
indehiscent **2**: *35*
Indian grass **4**: 43
Indian hemp **5**: 35
Indian kale *see* yautia
Indian pipe **3**: 41
Indian snakeroot **5**: 42
indicator species **7**: 12–13
indoleacetic acid (IAA) **3**: 12
indusium **7**: 38, *38, 39*, 40, *40,*
inflorescence 1: 28, 31, **2**: 9, <u>12–15</u>, *12–15, 18*, 20, *20*, 33, **9**: *15*, 24, *31*
globular **10**: *31, 32*
see also capitulum; flower
inhibitor **3**: 14–16
insect pollination *see* pollination
insect-egg mass slime **6**: 16
insecticide **10**: 41, 46
internode **1**: 10–11, *10*, 28, *28*, **2**: 46, **9**: *4*
and plant shape **1**: 11
interphase **1**: 16, *16*
intine **2**: 16, **8**: 6, *7*
inulin **10**: 46
involucre **10**: *47*
ipecac **5**: 42
Iridaceae 9: <u>28–29</u>
iris **1**: 33, 37, *37*, **2**: *13*, 34, 37, 47
family 9: <u>28–29</u>, *29*
Irish moss **6**: 21, **7**: 9
iron **3**: 10, *30*, 31, 32
ivy **1**: 23, *23*, 27, 41, **2**: *18*
poison **4**: 30

J

Jack fruit **5**: 10, 21, *22*
Jamaica pepper *see* allspice
japonica **9**: *5*, **10**: 26
jelly club, ochre **6**: *47*
jelly fungus (jelly) **6**: *38, 39*
Jerusalem artichoke **5**: 27, 28
Jew's ear **6**: *38, 39*
joint fir **5**: 42, **7**: 46–47, *46*
Juncaceae 9: <u>44–45</u>
juncio **9**: 44
juniper **5**: *38*, 46, **8**: 6, <u>46–47</u>, *47*
alligator **8**: 47
ashe **8**: 47
Bermuda cedar **8**: 47
Chinese **8**: 46, *47*
common **8**: 46, *47*
red (pencil) cedar **5**: 46, **8**: 47, *47*
Rock Mountain **8**: 47
Spanish **8**: *47*
western **8**: *47*
Juniperus **8**: <u>46–47</u>
jute **5**: 34–35, *35*

K

kale **5**: 20, *20*, **10**: 20
kangaroo-paw **2**: 24
kapok **5**: 31, *35*
karri gum **5**: 44
keel **2**: *4*
kelp **4**: 27, **6**: 14, 26–28, *28*
kenaf **5**: 35
Kew Seed Bank (UK) **2**: 30
kingdom **1**: 7
knotweed, Japanese **4**: 47
kohlrabi **5**: *20*, 21
kola nut **5**: *14*
kumquat **10**: 36

L

labellum **9**: *17*, 18, *18*
lady-of-the-night **10**: 40
lady's mantle **10**: 28
Lamiaceae 10: <u>42–43</u>
lamina **1**: *10, 38, 39*, **3**: *17*
laminarin **6**: 26
lantana, common **4**: *47, 47*
larch 4: 38, **5**: 44, 46, **8**: *4*, <u>26–29</u>, *27, 28*
Daurian (Dahurian) **8**: *27*, 28
Dunkeld **8**: *27*, 28
European **8**: 26–27, *27*
Japanese **8**: *27*, 28
manna **8**: 28
Siberian **8**: 28
Sikkim **8**: 26
tamarack (eastern; hackmatack) **8**: 27–28
western **8**: 28
Larix **8**: <u>26–29</u>
latex **10**: 34
laurel **4**: 28
ground **10**: *23*
white **10**: 7
lavender **10**: 42
laver **6**: 21, *21*
leaching **4**: 21
leaf 1: *10, 10*, 14, 28, 32, 38–43, *38–43*, 44, **3**: *6*, **7**: *18*, 19, **9**: *4*
abscission **3**: *13, 17*
air blisters **1**: 43, **3**: 8
aquatic species **1**: 41
arrangement **1**: 10, 41, *41*
axil **1**: 10, *10*, 28
blade **9**: 12, 14, *15*
bud **1**: 11, 28, **3**: 12, **10**: 6
cacti **10**: 14
classification **1**: 40–41, *40–41*
coleoptile **1**: 45
color **1**: 42–43, *42*, **3**: 8, *8*, 30–32, *30, 31*, 36
compound **1**: 40, 41, **10**: *27, 32, 39*
conifers **8**: 4, 6, 10
dicots **9**: 9, **10**: 4
evolution **6**: 8
fronds *see* frond
hairs **1**: 42, 43, **3**: 44, *44*, 49
lanceolate **1**: 40, **9**: 47
meristem **1**: 46–47
monocots **9**: 9, 10

Further Reading   Volume 7: Mosses and Ferns

Five Kingdoms. An Illustrated Guide to the Phyla of Life on Earth by Lynn Margulis and Karlene V. Schwartz. W.H. Freeman and Company, 1998.

Peterson Field Guides: Ferns and Their Related Families by Boughton Cobb. Houghton Mifflin, 1984.

The Ferns and Their Allies/The Mosses and Liverworts (The How to Know Series). Carolina Biological Supplies, 2000.

Useful website addresses

Worldwide Museum of Natural History
www.wmnh.com/mel0000.htm

(on rainforest ferns):
http://rainforest-australia.com

Ferns For Ever
http://home.tampabay.rr.com/
carrollpspace/ferns.htm

Ferns of Hawaii
www.lam.mus.ca.us/lacmnh/
departments/research/botany/wilsonferns/

(on tree ferns):
www.interpac.net/~artsmith/treeferns/

Plant Kingdom– Ferns and allies
www.perspective.com/nature/plantae/
ferns.html

Plant Kingdom–Mosses and allies
www.perspective.com/nature/plantae/
ferns.html

(on *Welwitschia*):
http://daphne.palomar.edu/wayne/
welwit.htm

Ginkgo Petrified Forest State Park
www.tcfn.org/tctour/parks/ginkgo.html
www.parks.wa.gov/ginkgo.gtm

(on ginkgos):
www.albion.edu/plants/
GINKFAMS.HTM

(on club mosses):
www.albion.edu/plants/
LYCOFAMS.HTM

(on ferns):
www.albion.eduíplants/
FERNFAMS.HTM
www.albion.edu/plants/
OPHIOGLOSSOPSIDA.HTM

(on whisk ferns):
www.albion.edu/plants/
PSILOFAM.HTM

(on horsetails):
www.albion.edu/plants/
SPHEFAMS.HTM

(on cycads):
www.albion.edu/plants/
CYCIMG.HTM

(on gnetophytes):
www.albion.edu/plants/
GNETFAMS.HTM

Picture Credits   Volume 7: Mosses and Ferns